APOCALYPSE
THE SECOND COMING

A Novel by
Derek Savage

Blessed is he that readeth,
and they that hear the words of this prophecy,
and keep those things which are written therein:
for the time is at hand.

APOCALYPSE
THE SECOND COMING

Chapter 1

The sun blazed in the sky as Brandon Summers drove swiftly down the street, racing over the asphalt with speed that shouldn't be present in this environment. Once he realized how fast he was going, he gripped the steering wheel of his sports car and downshifted to a lower gear, slowing the auto to a safe speed.

Then the most important element impacted his thoughts. He quickly scanned the area to be sure no kids were playing in the street. That would be the worst thing he could imagine. To be hauling-ass down a road, just caught up in the power of the engine rumbling so gracefully beneath his body, and crash into a child.

Accident or not, Brandon knew it would be unforgivable, a black cloud of shame that would haunt his soul for eternity. After confirming the coast clear, he shook his head and realized he had to be more observant before cockiness or misfortune came back to haunt him.

Glancing in the rearview mirror, he saw his own reflection staring back - a good-looking man in his early thirties with strong facial features, light colored hair, and gentle eyes that glistened with an array of hope. Most importantly, he saw a man that has a good heart.

Brandon rolled down his window to wave his arm outside. He loved when the wind danced attentively over the hairs on his skin. It always brought a touch of life to his spirit, a feeling of freshness. As a child he would spend hours playing in the sun, basically doing nothing, but in his mind he was helping the world to flourish by the attention he gave to its surroundings.

Brandon looked at the cloudless sky and entertained thoughts of going to the beach. It was so relaxing when waves splashed on the sand and the smell of Mother Nature drifted endlessly. Except common sense took control. He knew that Lisa, the passion of his life, would kill him if he went there without her. But fair was only fair. He wouldn't care for her to visit the beach without him, so he better not go there without her.

A smile crossed his face; he could feel he was maturing. The first step being that he cared for someone else's feelings more than he cared for his. It had taken years to reach this point, and now he could truly state he was approaching a manhood that would make his parents proud. He had reached a point of where he felt good about himself: the ultimate feeling of self-happiness and self-worth.

His favorite song on the radio ended, and it was perfect timing because he was pulling into the parking garage of the building where he worked.

After parking and strolling through the lobby, Brandon headed to the fourth floor and entered the Appleblum Insurance Company. Once he stepped into the office, he said hello to the receptionists and headed to his office. The moment he had a seat, he immediately noticed a red envelope sitting on his desk. What could this be? So he ripped it open and found a sweet surprise - the commission check from a large policy he wrote along with a note from his boss. "Great job, Brandon! Keep up the good work."

What a terrific way to start the day! He had to share his good fortune with his best friend and coworker, Matt, and hurried to his office.

Even though Matt's door was closed, there was no deterring Brandon as he rushed in without knocking.

Matt barely glanced up. He was too consumed in a sheet of the lamest business leads he had ever encountered.

"Hey, buddy. Guess what this is," Brandon stated while fanning the red envelope.

Matt gestured, "I hope it's your termination papers for rushing in here like a wild animal."

"Well, if I'm a wild animal then I'm a lion because this is the commission from the million dollar policy I wrote last week."

"You got lucky. I don't know how you got a thing off these leads."

"You call it luck, but I call it party time tonight!"

"Then drink a cold beer for me. I could use one right now if you know what I mean."

"Then I'll drink two. And don't sweat it, you'll write a big deal soon. But I have to call Lisa, see you later."

Brandon headed back to his office and dialed a familiar number. After two rings, a sensuous voice filled his ear, "Hello, this is Lisa."

"Hi, pretty lady. How are you?"

"I'm okay, and thanks for asking. What are you doing?"

"Just hanging at the office. Thought I'd call to give you some good news. Guess what happened."

Lisa could hear the tone in his voice. "There's no telling with you, so tell me."

His delivery was smooth. "I hope you're ready to have fun. I just got a fat paycheck so let's play hooky and get naked."

"I can't do that."

"Why not?" he pleaded.

"Because I have to work."

"That's no fun! But since I figured that'd be your response, here's my backup plan. Why don't we be adventurous and visit the shopping center tonight?"

"That's a wonderful idea! And since it's so pretty outside we should go to the Santa Monica Mall. We can even take a walk on the boardwalk first. We haven't done that in ages."

"Wow, we have the same vibes happening! I was thinking about the beach about an hour ago, so that's perfect. Get ready for a great time and I'll see you at home after work. Love ya."

"Love you back," Lisa responded happily.

\#   \#   \#

Seagulls drifted in the cloudless sky while hundreds of people crowded the sidewalks. Brandon and Lisa were driving down Main Street heading to the beach as Lisa stared at the blue sky. "This is such a pretty evening for the beach."

"That's why I'm taking you. I only wish it was earlier so you could've worn your new bathing suit."

"You're funny."

"I don't think seeing you in a sexy bikini is funny. In fact, I think it's a fantastic idea!" He smiled as he turned up the radio. The newscaster was announcing, "In the evening's news, terrorists explosions have erupted simultaneously in Baghdad, Saudi Arabia, and Jerusalem, turning all three areas into a killing zone. The dead have reached 247, with 968 wounded. ISIS has claimed responsibility for the bombings. Now to our local news. Two drive-by shootings have claimed four lives in..."

Brandon turned off the radio while shaking his head. "What's happening nowadays? It's like the world is getting crazier every day."

"Just yesterday a lady from my office was robbed in front of a restaurant. Some man jumped out from nowhere, stuck a butcher knife to her stomach and took all her money."

"Oh, my God, that's terrible! Did she get hurt?"

"No, she was very lucky. Some people happened to leave the restaurant and it scared the guy away."

"Now that was lucky. You know, it's becoming a full time job just to be safe anymore, and you never know when your number is up. Just like that some punk can kill you."

"That's so true. I wish I had an answer," she stated softly.

Brandon was thankful to have Lisa. She gave him hope and direction that made him feel good. "There's one thing I know for sure. At least we have each other."

Lisa adored the remark. Her man always knew the right words to say. "What am I going to do with you?"

"You'd be rich if you knew that answer," he chuckled.

"Being rich might be fun, but what will I spend all the money on?"

"That answer is simple, whatever your heart desires. And you better hold on because the beach is only a couple blocks away." As

6

Brandon punched the gas, Lisa grabbed the side door handle and they zoomed down the street.

# # #

Strolling hand in hand down the boardwalk, Lisa and Brandon were watching waves splash on the sand. It was so peaceful. Lisa breathed deeply, loving every bit of fresh air.

Brandon nudged her gently. "The sand sure looks inviting. Come on, sweetie." The instant they stepped in the sand, he kicked off his shoes and dug his toes downward. "Oh, this feels marvelous! Take off your shoes."

Lisa gladly took off her shoes and dug her toes into the velvety sand. It felt simply incredible after wearing high heels all day at work. "This does feel good!"

"Of course, it does. I'll never steer you wrong. Now how about a walk by the water and then we'll head to the mall?"

Lisa nodded her head joyfully. She loved the affection he delivered. While they moseyed down the beach, the glistening waves captivated her, but another sight stole her attention. A major storm was brewing miles away over the ocean. Ominous dark clouds were spinning from the inside out. She pointed. "Look at that storm, Brandon. Those clouds look like they're actually on fire."

"Good golly, where did that come from? It was a beautiful blue sky just seconds ago." He bumped his hip against hers, which made her smile. "Well, that's out there and we're right here, so let's enjoy this fine evening."

"Okay." But as they continued their walk, Lisa glanced once again at the menacing clouds. The sight gave her an eerie feeling, making her smile fade into concern.

# # #

As the sun set behind the mountains, Brandon and Lisa drove into the shopping center's parking lot. Fortunately it didn't take long to find a space. They found one near the front and parked.

Leaning over the console, Brandon rubbed his hand over her leg. "Here we are at the mall, or should I say the ladies playground." They shared a laugh while getting out of the vehicle, and he looked her over from head to toe. "Since you're looking so fine, it's your choice what we do first. Would you like to go eat at your favorite Chinese place or do a little shopping?"

She snuggled beside him. The warmth of his body sent chills surging through her. "I want to go shopping."

"I think that can be arranged." Lacing his arm around her waist, they strolled casually to the large glass door, which he immediately opened. "Let me open the door for the lady."

As Lisa stepped past him, she rubbed her body seductively against his. "You are being sweet this evening. There may be some sugar in store for you later on."

"There better be because big daddy is getting hungry." They entered the store, radiating joy.

After shopping for a brief period, Brandon picked out a couple shirts while Lisa chose a bottle of eloquent smelling perfume. They stepped to the sales desk near the front entrance of the store and placed their merchandise on the counter. Brandon inquired, "Is that all you want?"

"Yeah, this is perfect."

"Okay. Just making sure."

Perhaps Lisa spoke too soon. Directly beside their items was a glass display case that contained several strikingly attractive crystal pieces. Lisa's eyes sparkled when she saw one in particular. She opened the case and took out a perfectly carved crystal angel. "Look, honey. Isn't this pretty?"

The moment Brandon glanced over, a bright flash from a ceiling lamp shined on the glass object giving it a radiant glow. "That is nice."

"Can I have it?"

He smiled while pointing his right finger at his cheek. "I'll make you a deal. Plant one right here and it's yours."

8

"I'll take that deal," she remarked and kissed him gladly. As she stared at the angel, the words flowed from her lips, "This can be our guardian angel."

"If that makes you happy."

Suddenly, a loud commotion erupted at the back of the store. A salesperson screamed, "Help! Stop those thieves."

Brandon looked up. Danger was approaching. "What the ..!"

Before he had a second to react, twenty young hoodlums were running towards them, each carrying armfuls of merchandise. It was a smash and grab free for all.

As the thieves ran to the front door, one bumped forcibly into Brandon, knocking him off balance.

Brandon staggered slightly, but swiftly regained his footing. "Stop, you punks!" he hollered, and then saw another kid running directly at him.

But Brandon was quick. He lowered his shoulder, preparing for contact, and at the precise moment he rammed full force into the thief's chest like a linebacker crashing through a defensive line. Except the blow inadvertently threw the assailant straight into Lisa.

The unexpected contact hurled Lisa backwards, flinging the crystal angel out of her hand. It spun high into the air, then the crystal piece plummeted to the tiled floor and smashed into a thousand slivers.

# # #

Outside, a change exploded in the atmosphere. Almost instantly, bolts of lightning pierced the sky as thunder quivered the evening. A flood of clouds rolled in, twisting and tumbling over the horizon, suffocating the stars and full moon like a killer choking the life from its victim.

Street lamps were swallowed by the haze, leaving the world in darkness.

Chapter 2

Standing motionless in the department store, Brandon and Lisa were still startled by what transpired. But thankfully things were settling down. Clothing racks scattered the floor as employees were straightening things back to normal, trying to restore peace back into their familiar environment.

Most of the customers had left but a few still remained, the ones who wanted to see the conclusion. The place was a disaster and luckily no one got hurt.

The clerk at the sales desk handed Brandon his change and a bag with their items. "I'm sorry for what happened, sir."

"Hey, it's not your fault. But thanks anyway." He took the bag, put his arm around Lisa and noticed a sadness shrouding her face. "Come on, honey. Let's get out of here."

As they approached the doorway, Brandon remembered they hadn't eaten. "After all the commotion, I totally forgot about dinner. Are you still hungry or would you rather get something at home?"

"I want to go home."

"Sure, we'll go now."

Lisa was heartbroken. "Our little angel broke."

The sorrow in her voice was easily recognizable. "Don't worry, baby. We'll find you another one. I promise," Brandon stated in the most soothing voice he could muster.

But the instant they stepped outside the mall, their attention was diverted. An unusual feeling surrounded them as murkiness filled the air. They glanced skyward. All light had vanished, leaving the horizon in complete obscurity. "Check out how dark it is. I wonder where all these clouds came from?"

Lisa searched the sky, puzzled. "I don't know, but it's eerie. Can we go now?"

"Of course, we can." They stepped briskly to the car while continuing to stare skyward. Brandon mumbled, "I can't believe how horrendous it's become."

# # #

As they drove home from the mall, an extreme wall of clouds plastered the road, even to the point where Brandon had to drive a mere fifteen miles per hour just to see the pavement.

Lisa pointed her finger skyward. "Look how foggy it is. I wonder if it's going to storm?"

"I don't know, I've never seen anything like this in my life. It's pure darkness outside. So what do you feel like doing? Go home where it's dry and cozy or stop somewhere to grab a bite to eat?"

"If you don't mind I'd rather go home where it's safe. These clouds are getting worse."

"You're right, my headlights aren't doing a thing to penetrate them. I hope it's not like this tomorrow, especially since it's Saturday."

While the clouds smothered the windshield, Lisa whispered, "I know. This is spooky."

Chapter 3

Sitting closely beside each other, Lisa and Brandon relished each others company as they relaxed on the couch watching television. It was early morning and they just finished a nice breakfast. Brandon felt fantastic. He rubbed his full belly with delight. "That was some good eating. I didn't think they made food that delicious anymore."

"I'm glad you liked it." Lisa loved that her man took pleasure in her cooking. It gave her satisfaction.

Except Brandon was feeling a bit frisky, so he kept the complements flowing. "But I want to know how I got to be so lucky? My woman is beautiful and she can cook too!"

"You're too much, already starting up," she laughed.

"Baby, I started up with you the second I woke up and every moment since." Brandon put his arm around her and they snuggled together.

On the television, the news station flashed previews of the upcoming Channel Eight News. An outdoor cam showed an extremely dark and cloudy day. A voiceover announced, "Hello, this is Paul Thompson. In our top story of the day, you are looking at a live shot of this mysterious weather. L.A.X. has had hundreds of cancellations. We will be going live to the airport, but first let's examine these clouds." The view changed to the newsroom with Paul asking his co-anchor, "I have never seen it so dark at this time of the day. How about you, Jennifer?"

Jennifer looked as beautiful as always but there was something different about her. It was her eyes. Tension filled them in a noticeable way. "No, I haven't, Paul. These clouds are unbelievable. It was a chilling experience driving to work this morning."

"I think it's time to clear this up. Let's go to Tony for the weather." Paul glanced to his right. "Tony, what is happening outside?"

Tony, a sharply dressed weather reporter stood in front of a map of America. He seemed puzzled as he waved his pointer across the surface of the map. "I'm embarrassed to admit but I don't have a clue to what's transpiring. In my twelve years as a meteorologist, I have never seen or heard of anything like this. It's amazing. And I hate to phrase it this simply, but it seems as though this is a freak of nature."

Tony swept his pointer from the East Coast to the West. "You can see by this map that the cloud bank covers the entire United States. But folks, that's only half of the story!" A satellite map of the world appeared behind him. Excitedly, Tony waved his pointer across the surface while continuing, "The satellite map shows that the entire earth is swathed in this blanket of clouds. It is truly astonishing!"

Tony paused for a second to stabilize his breathing. "To answer your question, Paul, this weather cannot be explained." He glanced at the camera to give the viewers his award-winning smile. "But I will guarantee this, there's a whole lot of weather in store for you in this hour. So don't go anywhere."

#   #   #

Brandon was intrigued. "This weather is crazy, we might get some rain after all. I think I better investigate this." He stepped to the window and opened the curtains to an astonishing sight.

Darkness had stolen the sky, turning daylight into night. "Hey, Lisa. Check this out. It's like a low budget scary movie outside."

"What in the world is happening out there? It's worse now than before. The weather has been so freaky lately. Do you think it's global warming?"

"I'm not sure, that's a great question. Do you remember the TV Special we saw? They say the arctic glaciers are melting and it might flood the world, but they never mentioned the sky turning black."

"I don't know what's going on, but I think you better sit over here where mama can protect you," Lisa suggested while patting the couch seat beside her.

"You know, it does look safer over there." Brandon smiled as he strutted to the couch and sat beside her. "I think it's going to storm today. And I'm talking about big time thundering and lightning."

Lisa cuddled against his warm body. "If that happens, then you'll have to protect me."

"Just so you know, I'll protect you from Heaven to hell and everywhere in between."

"You're so good to me," she purred softly.

"Of course I am, and that's because I love you." Their faces formed a union as they kissed affectionately.

# # #

A 747 airliner bobbled through the cloudbank in a river of turbulence. The shaking got so extreme that the two pilots were becoming apprehensive, even to the point of paranoia. The plane then jolted severely, tossing them in their chairs.

Rick, the chief pilot, glanced at his partner. "Why don't you make the announcement."

"Sure." He picked up the microphone. "Hello, ladies and gentlemen. This is Billy Hamilton, your copilot. As you can feel we are currently experiencing air turbulence. Please pay close attention to the safety lights and keep your seat belts fastened at all times. This cloudbank should be lifting shortly. Thank you for your patience and have a nice flight."

Billy placed the microphone back in its cradle. "I hope I was correct about the clouds breaking soon, I can't see a thing out there. Plus my computer isn't giving any type of a directional read out." Billy tapped his fingers against the monitor in despair.

Rick leaned forward in an attempt to see something, anything. Haze consumed the horizon. Now the clouds and headwinds were building to the point of slowing the airplane. "What in the world is happening? This cloudbank is actually slowing the plane. Perhaps we should contact Tokyo ground control for landing assistance."

14

"Roger that," Billy agreed. "Would you prefer to make the call or me?"

"I will." Rick grabbed the microphone. "Tokyo ground control, this is flight one-two-six. We have no visual and are having problems finding the beacon. Could you help guide us in by radar?"

The Tokyo ground controller responded, "Roger that, flight one-two-six. We will be happy to assist. Give us a few seconds to chart your route and we'll bring you into the lineup."

Rick smiled as he mumbled in satisfaction, "That's what I call Japanese hospitality." He felt more at ease, but a strong burst of wind turbulence suddenly jolted the plane so brutally it snapped his head backwards.

Chapter 4

Woven together like a piece of silk, Brandon and Lisa's body were entwined while they slept in bed. Lisa eyes were fluttering under her eyelids, showing she was deep in dreamland.

She envisioned herself floating down the street to their neighborhood church. As she slowed to a stop in front of the building to admire its beautiful architecture, she felt simply inspired. An elegant waterfall flowed near a marble staircase that led to a large wooden door.

Lisa drifted through the door into the chapel, which was full of people of all races and color. Everyone was sitting beside each other in friendship, in harmony.

A preacher stood in the middle of the platform with a large wooden Cross suspended high in the air above him. He waved his Bible, questioning, "Do you know the feeling of loneliness or hunger in your heart because it's not fulfilled? I know there are many people who will tell you that's how life should be, but it's not the truth. There is one way you can put the love and happiness in your heart that you deserve, and that one way is God!" Continuing, his delivery was eloquent, "As the Lord says, 'Whosoever therefore shall confess me before people, I will confess them before my Father which is in heaven.'"

The preacher raised his arm. "Everyone listen carefully, you must come forward and accept God so you don't experience the same torment that John the Disciple suffered at Patmos." He pointed directly at Lisa and proclaimed, "Lisa, your time is now to confess Jesus!"

Lisa shuddered in her dream. She awoke quickly. A sensation of bliss engulfed her as she spoke softly, "I do confess you."

Shaking her head to gain full consciousness, she pushed her lover. "Brandon, wake up. I had a strange dream. Wake up, now!"

With eyes half shut, he rolled over. "What is it, honey?"

"I had a dream that seemed so real. It told me to accept God and I did. And I want you to do it before it's too late."

"That's good," he mumbled sleepily.

"I'm serious, Brandon. It said to do it before you suffer like some disciple did."

Brandon glanced at the clock. "It's four o'clock in the morning! Who cares what those folks went through? We'll talk about it later. See you in a couple hours." He rolled over, going back to sleep.

But Lisa didn't go back to sleep. She lay in bed wondering what the people of the ancient world had endured.

#   #   #

Traveling back through time to the year 95 AD, wind roared across the rocky coastline of Patmos Island, encasing a work crew of prisoners in a tornado of sand. "Damn! Why did I ever take this nasty job? I must have been crazy. A couple extra denarius for this crap," an overweight prison guard hissed disgustingly.

Tiberius cursed the sun for baking his baldhead while he eyed the crew of twenty prisoners. All deadbeats! Perhaps he should torture every one of them to brighten his mood.

He stood on a small hill, savoring his power. In his right hand he held a wicked whip, the cat of nine tails, and admired the recent adjustments he made by adding several pieces of broken bone and rocks at the ends of the straps. This way it will rip the skin from the prisoner when they were smacked with it.

Tiberius loved to beat people.

The slave driver discovered that a strong whipping was the swiftest way to ensure that the prisoners would do exactly what they were told, or whatever he wished.

A strong gust of wind blew the leather straps against his thigh, giving him a feeling of sexual gratification. But Tiberius' enjoyment was short lived when he noticed an aging worker slacking at his

17

duties. This caused anger to surge through his veins, so he snapped the whip wildly and headed after the captive.

An old man clung to his pickax with the last of his strength, barely able to draw breath. The heat was sucking the life from him. He then noticed the guard running his way.

"What are you doing? This is not a rest break," Tiberius barked with hatred raging in his voice.

"Please, a second. I feel dizzy," he moaned. "I am old."

The elderly man's pleas had no effect. Tiberius didn't care if the prisoners lived or died, only that they suffered whenever he chose to make them do so. The guard raised his whip high and lunged at him. "I don't care how old you are."

"Please!" the old man wailed.

"I said, no!" The slave driver lashed the whip across the prisoner's back, causing him to scream out in pain. But the helpless cries only made Tiberius more sinister. "Shut your stinking mouth." Once again, he slapped his whip brutally across the man's back.

The prisoner plummeted to the dirt but devoted all his energy to concealing his pain. Not even a breath of air left his body. He had to hide his anguish, or more would be dispensed.

Disappointed at the lack of response, Tiberius kicked the old man harshly in the side hoping for a satisfying crack of the ribs. The man's scrawny body was tossed like a twig, skidding across the ground. Tiberius kicked at the dust. "Get back to work now." The prisoner was hardly worth the effort of lifting his foot again, so Tiberius stomped away feeling good about himself.

Two other captives, John and Isaac, were at the back of the group breaking rocks. Isaac stared repulsively at Tiberius. "I wish your God would strike him down for abusing that person."

"What good would it do?" John responded. "They'll only find someone else to take his place."

Isaac knew his friend was correct. "Yes, but I would love to see someone snatch that whip from his filthy hands and beat him unmercifully." Isaac smiled at the thought as he swung his sledgehammer against a rock, breaking it into several pieces.

John understood his friend's anger. There was no escape from Patmos. Death was the only way to gain freedom, and death usually

18

came from overwork or beatings. Then the guards threw the lifeless body on the backside of the island where birds devoured their flesh.

Except John had learned to cope. Well into his 80's, he had endured much in his life.

The heat of baked earth breached the prisoner's thin shoes like they were standing in a pit of hot coals. But there was work to be done or suffer the guard's wrath. So John leaned over to pick up a rock and accidentally tripped on a jagged stone.

As he began to tumble, Isaac noticed this and instinctively reached out to help break the fall. He didn't want his buddy to get hurt in any way. John possessed a uniqueness that he had never seen before; there wasn't a person he admired more.

Regrettably, Isaac's effort to help his friend caught the guard's attention.

Rage flared through Tiberius when he saw the slaves slacking in their duties, yet he enjoyed it fully. It replaced the dullness of the hot day with the thrill of inflicting pain to others. He yelled sadistically and headed after them, "Get back to work, you old men!"

While the two stood to their feet, they noticed the guard hurrying their way with his whip in hand. Isaac knew a brutal beating was approaching unless he begged his way out of it, so he pleaded, "Please, he fell down. It was an accident. We will get back to work."

Tiberius was undeterred, but fortune intervened. A loud noise at the other side of the camp acquired his interest. Stopping in his tracks, Tiberius slapped the cat of nine tails across his hand. "Get back to work now or I'll whip you hard, you sorry old men." A growl reverberated from his throat as he returned to his post on the hill.

Isaac kept his sight focused on Tiberius, then he glanced at John. "I'm a prisoner on this island of hell because I killed a Roman soldier. You're a prisoner because you are a disciple of this Jesus of Heaven." Isaac swung his hammer to break a rock as he continued, "Is all of this worth it?"

Sweat was dripping down John's dusty face, but he was quick to respond, "Yes it is, for I am nothing without Christ."

Isaac took a moment to phrase his next question properly. "If you don't mind me asking, why does your God leave you here to undergo this torment?"

The question struck John like a prizefighter had punched him in the face. Hesitating for a second to gather his thoughts, he stated, "I don't have an answer because I don't have that knowledge. But I know there's a plan for me, I know there is."

"I hope you're right, my friend. If not, you will die here soon."

Chapter 5

Tiberius stood proudly on his small hill of dirt as he snarled at the group of prisoners. He hated them so much, but he had to feed them, so he bellowed out a call for the noon meal.

John was holding a heavy stone and dropped it to the dirt. "The older I become, the harder this work gets."

Isaac grinned at his friend's humor while he brushed his grimy shirt, causing dust and sweaty mud to flake away.

They both shared a laugh while gathering with the other prisoners. But Tiberius broke their pleasant thoughts by screaming from his hill, "Hurry up! If it was up to me, you would starve to death." The guard snapped the whip's leather straps in the air. "Since the Roman Government requires that I give you prisoners prayer time on Sunday, you have one hour. Then you'll be mine!"

As Isaac stared at Tiberius, thoughts of throwing him into a blazing fire soared through his mind. "I wish him straight to the fiery pits of Gehenna. He deserves hell and I'd love to see him burn alive. Just to witness his body set ablaze and his skin melting would fulfill me for life."

"Wish that not to anyone, he shall receive his due," John stated wisely.

"Then I hope he receives it soon!" Isaac responded wrathfully.

They watched Tiberius walk away. John felt sympathy for the guard's soul from knowing the future that awaited him. The punishment of everlasting hellfire, an eternity of extreme anguish.

But Isaac entertained a different thought, the thought of catching Tiberius behind a rock one evening and stabbing a knife into his neck, then slicing out his throat. Somehow this mental picture of blood gushing from Tiberius' body seemed to comfort him in a soothing way. "Let's get some grub."

21

In unison, the two men stepped to the ration line holding their clay bowls outward.

John waited patiently for his daily rations, hoping for a nutritional meal.

Unfortunately, immediate disappointment was the main dish. The server slopped a cup full of mush into his bowl, splashing it over the sides of the clay container. John's heart dropped. "Is this all? Is there no more?"

The server laughed boastfully. "Is there more for you? Sure there is." The cook rubbed his fat belly and burped loudly into John's face. "Breathe deeply because there's your dessert. Now get the hell out of here!"

The horrid smell sickened John. Something terrible had to be rotting in the cook's stomach. In a fast pace, John scurried from the table to get some fresh air. Anything to breathe again, anything.

Isaac followed after getting the same slop. "Where do you want to sit? Our food is getting cold."

"What do you mean our food is getting cold? Have you had a hot meal on this island yet?" Even though they knew the answer, they both grinned and found a seat on some rocks several feet from the group. Sometimes it felt great to get away from the others. Even a few extra feet brought some satisfaction.

John shifted his weight from side to side on the rock that served as his chair, but couldn't find a comfortable position.

Then it hit him.

He looked at his bowl of mush and knew this slop couldn't satisfy his true needs, so he handed the bowl to Isaac. "Here, take this. I am not hungry. It is yours."

Isaac heard the tone in his friend's voice and took the saucer without question. John stood. "I need to pray." He walked a short distance, kneeled and glanced skyward with his tired, humble eyes. "Lord, what do you have planned for me? If nothing, I shall die here soon."

The instant those words left his lips, a massive earthquake struck with such power it slammed him to the ground. He struggled with all his might to regain his composure, then John stood and looked outwards toward the ocean.

John was witnessing an astonishing sight. Carpets of clouds were tumbling inside out as they rolled in over the coast, quickly swallowing the land of Patmos in a dark haze.

John was defenseless, and then something strange happened. The clouds started to swirl around him, spinning swifter and swifter to the point of building up a suction of force that pulled him upwards.

With no way to stop the motion, John began to tumble head over heals flying through the black clouds. The whirlwind was somehow pulling him into heaven, and then he slowed to a stop.

Totally amazed, John looked around and saw an enrapturing sight. As far as he could see white fluffy clouds coated the horizon in pure beauty.

Suddenly, a loud voice thundered from behind, "I am Alpha and Omega, the first and the last. Which is, and which was, and which is to come, the Almighty."

John froze in fear. What was happening? What should he do? The presence that surrounded him sensed his panic and laid a hand upon his shoulder. "Fear not, I am he that liveth and was dead; and behold, I am alive for evermore: and I have the keys of hell and of death."

A wave of fright forced John to close his eyes tightly, but he found enough courage to open them once again. A shining image stood before him, an image that made warmth flood his spirit. "My Lord, is it you?"

"Yes, John. I am he."

John was stunned. It was all so incredible. It was Jesus, the person he had lived beside, the one who performed all the miraculous miracles. Except he looked entirely different.

Christ had the appearance of the ultimate warrior. His face and hair were shining fiercely as his eyes were like piercing lasers jutting from his soul.

The brightness was too intense for John. It was obvious this wasn't the meek person he had once lived alongside. John bowed his head. He didn't know what to do or what to say. This was too much for him to absorb is such a short period of time.

The mighty voice thundered, "John, I have chosen you to deliver my message unto the seven churches and to the world." Instantaneously, an antique scroll materialized before him.

A million thoughts suddenly dominated John's mind. What was inside the scroll? Could the meaning of life be written or the future shown? Could it explain the secrets of God? Or was it empty?

Before he concluded any answer, he was told, "Write these things which you have seen. These are the things which are, and the things which shall take place hereafter."

Jesus pointed above them. "Look."

John stared upwards in amazement. A gigantic door appeared from nowhere, just floating in space. Then the door began to open and the throne of God was revealed. Christ commanded thunderously, "Appear."

A huge angel stepped through the doorway and stretched his arms to John. "Come up hither. I will show you prophecy that must take place."

John looked on in bewilderment, but further explanation was immediate. "For heaven has been opened unto you. Go, see, and be a witness of what shall happen." Right as John grabbed the antique scroll, he was swept into the throne with the mighty angel, vanishing out of sight. They disappeared into the Kingdom of Heaven.

Chapter 6

Dark clouds covered the sky above the Shady Tree Meadows graveyard. Herman, the grounds keeper, overweight and unshaven, placed squares of grass on a fresh grave. "Damn clouds, I can't see what I'm doing down here." He tossed another square of grass on the freshly turned dirt while speaking sensuously, "Here you go, baby, let Hermy cover you up." Herman grinned sordidly.

Since it was early Sunday morning and he hated to work, or bury people on the weekend, he decided to take a break. He could feel his true passion bulging in the pocket of his overalls, and it sent a burst of anticipation through his body.

Herman pulled out a pint bottle of cheap whiskey, his favorite, the "Famous Times" brand, and quickly unscrewed the lid to take a large swig.

As the liquor flowed down his throat, he stared lustfully at the grave. "Yeah, sweetheart. It's a shame you never got a chance to meet me. I would've shown you what a real man is like."

Herman took another swig and coughed, spitting it all over the place. "Shit, what a waste of good whiskey! Done got myself all wet." He smirked at the grave. "Just like I would have gotten you, baby. All wet!"

A sick laugh echoed from his throat as he studied the headstone. "But your type wouldn't like me anyway. You must be some rich person to afford one of these fancy gravestones."

The gravestone was a perfectly chiseled rock that showed an illustration of Jesus. Below that was the picture of a lovely woman in her forties. "Mary Jo Williams. Born an angel. May she rest in Heaven."

This confirmed Herman's suspicion. "Now I know you're some rich person. All you rich people are the same, just don't care about anybody but yourselves. To hell with you and your fancy Jesus gravestone."

# # #

In the throne, John looked in every direction to analyze his new surroundings. He had to catch his breath. The beauty that flourished around him was overwhelming. The sky was aflame with the most breathtaking colors he could ever imagine.

Directly before him, not even hundred feet away, was a golden chair wrapped in sparkling jewels.

This was the altar of God. The Spirit of God sat boldly in the golden chair as lightning bolts exploded thunderously above.

Beside the throne were seven golden lamps that blazed of eternal flames, and sitting in front of the throne in a horseshoe shape were the twenty-four elders. Each one clothed in a pure white robe with a crown of gold on their head.

Located in the middle of everything was a sea of glass, an ocean of clear crystal. Waves were pouring forth from the crystal lake like a volcano had erupted beneath the surface.

John then focused on the four living beasts that guarded the throne, and they were enormous in size and stature.

The first beast resembled a lion, the second a calf, the third beast had the face of a man, and the fourth was like an eagle. Each beast had six wings, three on a side, and the wings were entirely full of eyes. This allowed them to see and be aware of everything.

John stated in pure awe, "The throne of God!"

The angel beside him nodded his approval. "Thou has spoken well."

John knew this had to be a dream. It couldn't be real. An actual angel stood beside him who was assigned to show him these things, and the angel was gigantic.

"Oh my, he's big. He must be a warrior angel," John wondered aloud.

"That is correct. I am a warrior," the angel stated powerfully.

The response caught John completely off guard. He immediately knew this wasn't a dream. "I believe it, I can certainly see why."

26

He put his head down, then a loud noise from the altar diverted his attention and he noticed several angels flying in the sky.

John felt that something enormous was about to occur, but he was lulled by a sense of contentment. He knew that the entire army of God was on his side.

The Spirit in the exquisite chair twisted fiercely as the four beasts and twenty-four elders watched in anticipation. Then the most intense voice of all creations rumbled, "The time is at hand to bring my children home."

At that moment, four angels carrying golden trumpets flew down from the upper heavens. The Spirit commanded, "Blow your trumpets. The time is now!"

As John wrote these events in the scroll that he received earlier, his mind was racing to think of a proper title for this book. Then the name "Revelation" impacted his thoughts.

# # #

Standing in the Shady Tree Meadows, Herman was staring at Mary Jo's impressive gravestone as Jesus' picture glared back at him. Herman shook his head in disgust. These filthy rich people could afford a fancy headstone, but his parents had to be buried with a plain rock as theirs. So he wanted to show Mary Jo what he thought of her expensive grave.

Herman cleared his throat, hocked up a mouthful of lung sludge and spit at the headstone.

His salvia soared in the air, splattering dead center in Jesus' face. "Damn right, that's what I call a perfect shot," Herman bragged boastfully, happy with the precision of his aim.

But at that very instant, things changed dramatically. The dark clouds above started to thrash turbulently. Blowing back and forth, they were whipping through the sky. Then bolts of lightning thundered and an earthquake shook so powerfully it could have awakened the dead.

Herman stood wobbly in the graveyard. He looked everywhere, dumbfounded. "What the hell just happened?" he yelled.

Inside their bedroom, Brandon and Lisa were getting ready for a nice evening out on the town. It was their date night, and they always tried to make that happen at least twice a month. As Brandon put on a shirt, Lisa slid on a tight black dress. He couldn't believe his eyes; she looked stunning. "You look absolutely gorgeous. My better half is one sexy mama!"

"You're too much," she said playfully.

"When it comes to you, yes I am." A distant rumbling gave a brief warning just before the apartment shook hard, rattling odds and ends on the dresser. "What was that?"

"I don't know. It was probably an earthquake. We are in Los Angeles," Lisa replied matter-of-factly.

"Yeah, but I don't think it was an earthquake. I think it was my hunger for you that shook this whole building," Brandon purred.

"You're crazy. I should throw you in a cold shower."

"That sounds fun. In fact, I would love it. Let's take that shower now!"

"Be quiet, Lover Boy, and get ready so we can leave."

"Yes, ma'am." Brandon grinned while tucking his shirt into his pants.

Chapter 7

The Vice President stood proudly in his White House office by a large window, watching it rain outside. He despised the sight. "Damn rain, I was supposed to go golfing today!" His intercom buzzed, pulling his attention. He pushed the speaker button. "What is it?"

"Mr. Vice President, Clergyman Father Jack Smitty is here for your eleven o'clock meeting."

"Then show him in."

"Yes, sir. Right away." Within a moment, Father Smitty entered the office. "Hi, Jeff. How's your day?"

"Nasty, that's how it is! Just look at this weather. It killed my golf game."

"Well, there's always a bright day in store for you tomorrow," Smitty responded with a plastic smile gleaming on his face.

Jeff stared at him. "What do you mean? Do I look like one of those fools who sit and listen to your sermons?"

Smitty shrugged, "Just trying to be helpful. So to what's important, have you thought about our conversation?"

"Of course, and its already in motion."

"That's what I wanted to hear!" Smitty smiled mischievously as thoughts of his next move entered his mind.

#   #   #

In the streets of Tokyo, Japan, people stared in astonishment at the turbulent clouds that railed in the sky. Some stood motionless, confused, as others ran in panic.

The clouds stopped abruptly, which brought some clam to the chaos. But that changed quickly as a bolt of lightning rippled thunderously and the clouds were sucked into heaven, leaving the horizon in a bright blue.

Mobs of people gasped and then a stampede exploded. Walls of human flesh moved blindly down the streets, trampling over anyone that had the misfortune of falling.

An older woman got knocked to the ground like a rag doll. Masses stomped over her, kicking her brutally in the side. She screamed for help but a foot crashed into her face, bursting her nose. Dark red blood shrouded her face.

As pain attacked her, she saw a sight in the sky that frightened her even worse than being stomped to death. "Nanda, Nanda??" she yelled, "What's that??"

# # #

In Mexico City, an eerie hush fell over the streets. Crowds of people were watching the churning clouds disappear as the dark sky turned crystal clear.

Daylight now coated the world, delivering a clear view of all.

Then, from above, the sound of a trumpet blasted powerfully. Everyone gazed upwards in shock. Prophecy was evolving before their very eyes.

At that moment, Jesus Christ appeared. Clothed in pure white, he floated in the air and then sailed to the earth with his hair and robe whipping in the breeze behind him.

Christ suddenly came to a stop in the sky, hovering above every home, every city, and every nation. Somehow his image could be seen throughout the world.

Jesus opened his arms to give an invitation to all of his true children, a summons for them to spend eternity in paradise.

Confusion and pandemonium burst through the crowds, but many knew exactly what was occurring. They fell to their knees calling out joyfully at the revelation.

Behold, he cometh with clouds; and every eye shall see him.
Revelation 1:7

\#   \#   \#

Herman stood spellbound in the graveyard beside Mary Jo's grave. Clutching his whiskey bottle close to his chest, he hoped it could somehow protect him from the vanishing clouds.

Except his future was changing for the worst. A metal button on his overalls snagged his hand and this made him drop his bottle of liquor. "Shit," he grumbled and tried to look at it, but his head was snapped up forcing him to stare skyward. "What the hell?" he hollered and then saw Jesus hovering above.

The sight scared him tremendously. In a quick move Herman took off running as swiftly as his chubby legs could carry him, but he accidentally tripped over a shovel and fell flat to the ground.

With his eyes still focused to the sky, he screamed, "Holy cow!"

A loud rumbling began and the ground shook like an earthquake erupted, tossing Herman around like a fat bag of manure. He was completely terror-stricken, but his worst nightmare was transpiring right beside him. Several of the gravesites started to blow open. Dirt exploded upwards, uncovering the caskets for all to see.

Incredibly, the dead were being resurrected back to life. They floated miraculously out of their graves as their spirits and bodies were coming together into one, forming a glorified body.

Herman used every bit of energy his drunken body could conjure to save himself. But there was no escape. Then the grave in front of him blasted open, covering his body in dirt. He screamed in terror, but another grave blew open that threw dirt into his open mouth.

The gravedigger gagged for air. Dirt was clogging his throat, suffocating him. He quickly clawed at his neck to dislodge the muck from his windpipe, but it didn't work. So he beat his fist on his stomach to induce vomiting.

Almost instantly, alcohol and dirt heaved from his gut, plastering his face in half dissolved liquor and stomach acid. Herman gasped for air over the decaying smell. He tried to look around but the

31

vomit blinded him, so he wiped his eyes to clear his vision. That was when he noticed strange movement near his toes.

A woman was rising from the grave below.

Herman looked everywhere searching for some avenue to flee. There had to be one, there had to be. But there wasn't.

He was trapped in the center of it all.

As the once dead believers rose gracefully from their graves, they began to fly elegantly into the bright sky.

Herman stared at the bodies. They were not decayed to any degree. They looked as good, if not better, than when they were alive. Their clothes weren't even faded. But how could this be? Many of them had been dead for years. His Grandfather even buried some of them and that was over fifty years ago.

Herman blamed the cheap liquor for the hallucinations. What else could it be? But before he concluded an answer, he saw Mary Jo Williams rising out of her grave. She floated in the air before him.

Herman fell into sheer panic. He knew it was her. He assisted with her embalming and buried her body in the dirt.

Mary Jo hovered above her gravesite and stared into Herman's eyes. She saw extreme fear, but more importantly, she saw the look of no faith, something she hated to see.

She must try to calm his fears. Mary Jo stretched her arms towards him and spoke gently, "Find God and fear no more." She then floated to heaven along with the others.

The gravedigger finally realized this was actually happening. "Oh, shit!" he squealed frightfully.

At that instant, Herman's blood curdled in terror, bursting his heart inside his chest. The old drunk's head flopped over landing face first in the dirt.

For the Lord himself shall descend from heaven with a shout, with the voice of the archangel, and the trumpet of God: and the dead in Christ shall rise first.
1 Thessalonians 4:16

Chapter 8

In an attempt to pick up his pace so they could leave, Brandon rushed to the bathroom to finish the final touches. And he needed to finish quickly. Lisa was becoming impatient.

After squirting some toothpaste on his toothbrush, he stroked it across his teeth. Lisa called from the living room, "Aren't you ready yet?"

"I will be in a second." He rinsed out his mouth and spit, then hurried to the living room. "Here I am, baby. I'm all yours."

"It's about time! I've seen a turtle move faster than you are today."

"That must have been a quick turtle because I've been rushing." He stepped to the door. "Look, I'm already at the door. Now I'm waiting on you!"

She grinned as she grabbed her purse and they bolted out the apartment, completely unaware of the rapid changes developing in the outside world.

# # #

A gust of wind surged through an abandoned ghost town, ripping shingles from the roof of an old church. Tumbling downward, they landed in a graveyard located beside the building. But once the shingles hit the ground, dirt blasted from several of the graves.

Dead believers were beginning to rise, delivered to a life of eternal freedom.

Women were dressed in vintage clothing and many of the men wore banker's apparel. Now two cowboys rose upwards with their six shooters still in their holsters. One cowboy pulled his pistols, twirled them around his fingers and smiled happily. His gun spinning abilities brought back so many joyful memories of his ranch hand days.

# # #

All over the world, people of every race, color and from every country sailed into paradise. It was a beautiful composition of all coming together into a family of peace and love. A family of God.

At every location on the globe those left behind could look up and see the faithful dead disappear into heaven.

# # #

Inside the cockpit of the 747, the two pilots were completely thunderstruck by the sight. Thousands of bodies littered the horizon.

Rick, the chief pilot, looked closer out the windshield. "What is going on?"

The copilot, Billy, comprehended exactly what was transpiring. "Oh, sweet Jesus. It's the Rapture!"

At that instant, Billy disappeared out of the plane, swept up as were millions upon millions of others.

Rick searched the cockpit. It was empty. "What the hell?"

In the passenger area, a flight attendant was serving a glass of milk to a child. "Here you go, honey." The little girl took the glass, giggling, "I like milk, it gives me a white mustache." The child asked innocently, "Do you want to see it?"

The girl's mother interrupted sternly, "Leave the stewardess alone. She doesn't have time for your silly games."

The child's face fell. The stewardess winked at her to show her everything was cool. "It's okay, she isn't bothering me at all. In fact, I would love to see what a white mustache looks like."

The girl smiled as she took a huge sip of milk that covered her upper lip. She exclaimed happily, "You see it? I have a white mustache." They both giggled and then the child and stewardess

34

vanished, swept upwards into heaven. The tray of drinks smashed to the floor, splashing liquid all over the mother's face.

"My baby, my baby," the mother squealed. "Where's my baby?"

Another flight attendant stood dazed in the first class section. At least forty percent of the passengers and crew had vanished, like a magic wand had been waved over the plane.

Then the aircraft jolted to one side, throwing passengers throughout the cabin. The plane dropped rapidly towards the earth while screams of the doomed passengers filled the floating coffin, and they crashed to the ground in a fiery death.

Chapter 9

Riding the slowest elevator in the universe to the parking lot, Brandon leaned against the wall and stared at his lovely girlfriend. Lisa looked simply adorable in her tight black dress. "I think I'm with the finest looking woman in the whole world!"

"What are you up to?" she questioned.

"I'm not up to nothing. I'm just admiring you."

"Well, I guess that's okay."

The elevator doors opened. When they stepped out, Brandon tapped his front pocket and realized he didn't have his keys. "Darn, I have to go back upstairs. I left my car keys in the apartment."

"You'd forget your head if it wasn't attached. But don't worry, we'll take my car. It'll make us late for the movie if you have to go back upstairs. Let's go, Brandon!"

"Sounds like a deal. Right this way, pretty lady." Brandon grabbed her hand and they strolled casually to Lisa's automobile.

# # #

The clacking sound of balls crashing together echoed in the low light and smoky haze of a backwoods pool hall. Matt and another coworker, Steven, were shooting a game of pool.

Steven analyzed every inch of the table for his next shot. "Where's Brandon at today?"

"He took Lisa to the movies. Said he'll be here next week to take your money."

"Yeah, right. I can beat that boy blindfolded." Steven's next shot came into view. "Well, Matt, you better get that five dollars ready. I'm about to kick your butt in this game."

"You aren't going to kick anything. The best advice I can give you is to step away from that table and let a real man have a turn."

Steven leaned over the table and laughed. "A real man, huh?" Taking his shot, he knocked the seven ball into the corner pocket and walked around the table. "One down and one to go. Then it's the eight ball."

Matt didn't say a word. He knew the game could be near its end.

Steven shot again and knocked the two ball into the side pocket. "There you go, my friend. I believe that established exactly who the real man is here."

"That didn't establish anything, you got lucky. And what about the eight ball? It's still there. Where are you going to put that?"

Steven glanced over the table calculating every inch of the green surface. "You may have a point, I guess I really don't have a shot. But that's because all of your balls are in the way!"

"Oh, shut up," Matt retorted jokingly, even though it was the truth.

Steven waved his arm over the table pointing out his next, and hopefully, final shot. "Check it out. This is how it's coming down. Eight ball, one rail, corner pocket."

"Sure. If you make that I won't hesitate to pay you the five dollars," Matt told him confidently.

Steven rubbed some blue chalk on the tip of his stick, adjusted his body weight, cocked the pool stick and shot. The cue ball knocked the eight ball smoothly into the side railing. It then rolled gracefully into the corner pocket dropping out of sight.

"Thank you, sweet Jesus," Steven exclaimed delightfully. "There you go, just as smooth as silk. How about the five dollars you owe me."

Matt reached into his pocket. "That was a magnificent shot. Truthfully, I don't have a problem paying for that entertainment. But how about this? One more game, double or nothing."

"Now you sound like Brandon, and you know I can't. My wife is at home waiting for me. How about next week? I'll play you for double or nothing then."

"Oh, I understand. You don't want me to pay you now so you can hold it over me all week."

"Good try, but I didn't say that. I want my five dollars now! What I meant is I'll be generous enough to give you a chance to win it back next week."

Matt handed him the five. "Here you go. You won it fair and square."

"That's right," Steven commented while he snatched the cash from Matt's hand. "Thanks for the gas money, my bike will love you for it."

"I bet it will," Matt chuckled. "You hanging out for another cold one? It's on me."

"I better not. One is my limit, especially when I'm on the motorcycle." Steven glanced at his watch. "Aw, no. It's almost four o'clock. Katie will kill me if I'm late. Did I tell you my boy is pitching in the kid's baseball game tonight?"

"Almost every day for the past week," Matt chortled. "You better get out of here. The last thing I want is for your wife to be mad at me for holding you up."

"That's words of a wise man. I'll see you at work Monday and tell Brandon I'll talk to him later."

"Okay, buddy. Drive safely."

"You know I will. Take it easy." Steven threw his leather jacket over his shoulder and walked out the front door. Once it swung open, the pool hall was absorbed in glistening sunlight.

"All right, the clouds have left and it turned out to be a gorgeous day." Steven looked directly at his freshly polished motorcycle, which made a smile cross his face. It made him feel good when his bike was so shiny. "Here I come, baby. Your daddy is about to take you for a ride."

# # #

Driving down a wide country road, Steven's feet were kicked high on the pegs. His motorcycle was purring majestically between his legs as wind rumpled his hair, caressing him with the freshness of Mother Nature.

Trees were whizzing by, one after another, and he throttled the gas. The sun was beaming brightly and he longed to feel the warmth

38

on his face, so he leaned his head back. At that moment he saw an exquisite sight.

Steven saw his Lord.

Jesus appeared in the sky with his arms held open, staring directly into Steven's soul.

Love and fulfillment swallowed Steven's spirit. His prayers were answered. In the flash of light, he vanished off his motorcycle and was swept up into the sky.

As Steven rose into the air, he glanced back and witnessed his bike crashing on the ground. But it didn't bother him; it no longer had any meaning. It was just an object made of steel and rubber.

Instead, he saw what was of true importance. His beautiful wife and son were soaring upwards. They came together as a family and sailed into paradise to a life of everlasting bliss, a life together that could never be broken.

Then we which are alive and remain shall be caught up together with them in the clouds, to meet the Lord in the air: and so shall we ever be with the Lord.
1 Thessalonians 4:17

Chapter 10

Gripping the steering wheel, Lisa drove down the street going to the movies. Brandon noticed something in the sky and pointed upwards. "Hey, check it out, honey. There's an air blimp. I've never seen one in real life before."

Lisa spotted the blimp. "Isn't that cute. I've never seen one neither. There must be a sporting event somewhere."

"You know, that's right," Brandon recalled. "The Dodgers are playing a championship game today. I hope they win."

# # #

The horizon had become so clear it gave the air blimp pilots a perfect view of the baseball stadium. The only problem they experienced were the drunken passengers in the back. Ever since their corporate office started selling the rear seats to the highest bidder, most of their guests had been the loud mouth types.

Today's passengers were no exception.

As an announcement blared over the stadium's intercom introducing the championship game, the passengers jumped up and down yelling, "Yee-haw!"

The pilot, Mike Reed, looked into the rearview mirror. "It looks like we're stuck with some wild ones today."

Copilot, Kevin Banks, took a peek. "That's what I was afraid of. Do you know who his father is?"

"Oh, no," Mike sighed. "Not another rich spoiled kid. Who's his father, the Sheik of Bali Ralla?"

"Close, my friend. It's that rich oil tycoon out of Texas. I can't remember his name but he was on the cover of Time magazine a few weeks ago."

"I know who you're talking about, the guy with the big ears." Mike snapped his fingers trying to recall. "What's his name? You know, I can't remember. But I do know his boy was busted at the airport last month with several pounds of reefer. It was a major news story."

A tapping reverberated on the siding glass partition that separated the two compartments. Kevin opened the window. "Yes, sir. How can I assist you?"

Brett yelled in a drunken slur, "Who the hell are you calling 'sir' back here? You can call my daddy sir but don't call me sir. We're at a baseball game, this ain't a damn office. You boys like a drink of some good tasting whiskey up there?"

Mike glanced at Kevin. It was apparent this guy could become a problem. "Thank you, sir, but I'm afraid we'll have to pass on your kind offer. We would lose our jobs if we were caught drinking."

Brett took the bait. "Shoot, I'd hate to make somebody lose their job. Except there is one thing, you boys got a match? I need to fire up this fat joint." He held up a huge marijuana cigarette and shouted to his friends, "It's time to get toasted and watch some ass kicking sports, yee-haw!" They all joined in with an energetic hoot and holler.

Captain Mike took control of the situation. He yelled into his microphone, "Everybody, sit down, now!"

The volume caught everyone off guard. They sat like a pack of startled puppies. Mike laid it out sternly. "You guys were briefed on the rules of riding in this ship. This is not a clubhouse or a playhouse. This is a blimp. It can be extremely dangerous. So sit down and enjoy the game. By the way, there is absolutely no smoking allowed. What do you want to do, blow us up?"

Kevin closed the window as he chuckled under his breath, "Man, you sure told them. I couldn't have done that any better myself." They shared a laugh while Kevin asked a question he had often wondered. "Hey, Mike. Have you ever smoked any reefer?"

"Well, I tried it back in my college days, but I quit when I got married and that was years ago. How about you? I know you've smoked some of that wacky weed before."

Kevin confessed, "Well, you know how it goes being a single man and everything. Sometimes the lady folks like to have a little smoke so I'm not opposed to it. I even enjoy taking a puff occasionally, especially when I'm playing my guitar. But I haven't smoked it lately. Most of these churchgoing girls I've been dating don't indulge much. I guess it's God's way of telling me to slow down."

"Yeah, the Lord works in mysterious ways," Mike agreed wholeheartedly. As they smiled, both were Raptured and swept upwards into the blue sky.

Brett sat in the rear strategizing a way to smoke his joint. There had to be a way. All he wanted to do was get high and watch the game. Hell, he spent over twenty thousand dollars to ride in this blimp, which should at least buy him the privilege to smoke a joint.

He glanced at the back of the pilots' heads. They appeared to be having a good time and then they disappeared in the blink of an eye.

Brett shook his head. There had to be an explanation. The pilots probably bent over to tie their shoes. Yeah, that had to be the answer. So he looked at his friends to make sure his vision was clear. It was crystal clear. He saw his buddies taking a shot of liquor and talking crap about who could screw the chick in the dirty book the best.

Even though things appeared normal, Brett sensed something strange. He couldn't put his finger on it, so he glanced out the side window. The sight was staggering.

The stadium was half empty. How could this be? It was completely full only one minute prior. There was no way the arena could have emptied out that fast. It wasn't humanly possible. Brett searched his mind for an answer but came up blank. So he smacked the pilot's partition with his hand.

He received no answer.

Brett smacked it again. Still no response. How dare they ignore him? As anger consumed his spirit, he pressed his face against the glass to yell at the pilots for avoiding him, but the cockpit was empty. No one was flying the blimp. Brett screamed hysterically, "There's some voodoo shit happening here!"

# # #

A dad and his son sat inside the baseball stadium behind home plate. The man was excited. This was the boy's first live sporting event and it was a championship game, which equaled a fantastic way to spend the afternoon with his son.

It would have been a perfect day except for the greasy haired man that sat in front of them. From the moment they arrived he had been making rude and vulgar comments that weren't appropriate for the boy's ears.

The greasy haired man burped loudly. "That was one, now here comes two." He thrust his face forward and burped again. "That tasted nasty."

His friend looked on in disgust. "Shut up, Sal. You're about the rudest person I've ever met."

Sal took it as a compliment. "You know, Roy, that tasted like I vomited. No, that ain't it. That tasted as bad as my wife's cooking." Sal laughed at his own joke and took another swig of beer.

The child's father stared at the back of this crude oaf. It was a shame he couldn't keep his son from people like this forever, but he could put a lid on it for now. He reached his hand out and just before contact with the greasy person's shoulder, the father and son were swept upwards.

Soaring into the sky, the father glimpsed back at Sal and felt sorry for the wretched person. Then they passed the blimp and saw a very nervous guy trying to light a joint with a match.

The match sparked to life that ignited a helium leak, and the blimp exploded into a massive fireball.

Flames and fire flashed out consuming both the dad and boy, covering them completely in searing heat. But as the fire dissipated, neither one had a mark or a burn.

Dad exclaimed, "Son, look up and tell me what you see." The boy looked up. "Daddy, daddy, there's Jesus in the sky!"

As the words left the child's lips, they flew into paradise as the blazing blimp crashed into the center of the stadium, scorching the dome and all the people left behind in blistering heat.

# # #

In the middle of Missouri, twelve workers slaved in a field picking fruit and fighting off bees for no more than ten dollars an hour. At least it was work. Many of these people had a good heart. They knew that an honest dollar was worth far more than any amount of illegal money. So they worked and they worked hard. While picking fruit, six were Raptured and floated away in a flash.

The workers left behind froze in their tracks as a few pointed their fingers upwards at them, absolutely stunned. They all gasped. What was in store for them?

Then shall two be in the field; the one shall be taken, and the other left.
Matthew 24:40

# # #

A chain link fence divided two backyards in a nice suburban Virginia neighborhood. One side housed a mean pit bull, the other a sweet mellow collie. The pit bull was barking aggressively at the collie, clawing and tearing at the fence. But the collie didn't care. He was lying comfortably on the grass while ignoring the mean dog.

Then the earth shook viciously, throwing the pit bull to the ground. Except the collie had a different future in store. He began to float gracefully into the sky. In mid-stride, he turned and barked a farewell.

The pit bull immediately stopped barking as he stared upwards in confusion, scared into silence.

Chapter 11

Cruising down the street in Lisa's shiny car, they were passing the church that Lisa saw in her dream. She pointed. "Look, Brandon. There's the church I told you about, the one where the cool preacher called for me to accept God. Let's go there next Sunday."

"We might do that, but we better hurry if you want to see the movie. It starts in ten minutes and you always hate to miss the beginning. Perhaps now that you believe in Jesus, he can get us there quicker."

"Be quiet, Brandon. You shouldn't make jokes about things like that. And you should have driven," she snapped back.

"Yeah, you're right. I'm sorry, sweetie pie," he stated apologetically. Something big was on his mind and Brandon Summers couldn't hold it back any longer. He slipped her a hint. "The movie sounds fun but I can't wait until it's over. I have some special plans for us. And so you know in advance, it's going to be just you and me. I'll even drive. Maybe open the door for you, too."

"What are you talking about?" she asked curiously.

"I was thinking that after the show we'd go to Parsay's for dinner."

"Parsay's! That's the nicest restaurant in town. What's the occasion?"

"I have a special question to ask and I hope it makes you happy. I would tell you now but it's a secret, so you'll have to wait." Brandon grinned mischievously.

Lisa looked deeply into his eyes. Did he plan to propose? They have talked about it several times and she knew it would happen, but was this the night? Adrenaline surged in her veins as the sparkle in his eyes showed real commitment.

His eyes always gave him away; they were a shining vessel to his soul. As they smiled at each other, passion flowed in their hearts.

Brandon and Lisa shared a true bond of love, one that was so complete and binding. But there was another bond that was stronger, the bond with the Almighty.

In that very instant, Lisa vanished from the car and was Raptured into the sky.

Brandon freaked. What just happened? He yelled, "What the hell!"

No one was driving the automobile, which made it swerve into the oncoming lane. He was heading directly down the center lane of traffic.

Brandon grabbed the steering wheel with one hand and smacked her seat up and down with the other trying to find her. She had to be somewhere, she had to be. There was no way she could've vanished like that. It was impossible. "Lisa, Lisa!" he screamed in horror.

He looked at the backseat. Perhaps she was thrown there, even though there hadn't been a bump in the road that could've projected her rearwards. He had to look anyway, searching high and low.

Lisa was nowhere.

Brandon's heart sank. A bad feeling erupted in his stomach. Then an immense sound pulled his attention back to the road.

Another car was speeding straight at him. The automobile was empty. The driver must have vanished like Lisa. Brandon yanked the steering wheel to swerve out of the way to avoid an accident.

It was too late.

The car rammed forcibly into Lisa's automobile and this hurled Brandon's head into the passenger's window, shattering glass into a thousand pieces.

Thick blood poured down his forehead as the car slid into a curb, bringing the automobile to a screeching halt.

Brandon's eyes drooped shut. His body hurt to the extreme where he could barely move, but his mind still worked. And it was focused on the one thing of importance: Lisa.

Using the last of his strength, he stared out of the passenger window and witnessed a sight in the sky that made him quiver. Lisa was flying away with Jesus and thousands of others.

Jesus, Brandon thought, this has to be an illusion. The accident must have scrambled his brain. Right away he blinked his eyes several times to refocus.

He looked again.

This time he saw Lisa stop in midair. A concerned expression covered her face as she hovered there staring at him. He hoped that she would come back to save him. Perhaps she could float back, grab his hand and take him with her. That would be a great plan of action!

That didn't happen. She waved at him and disappeared with the others, leaving him alone, hopeless. Brandon's eyes fluttered. A feeling of dread clenched his gut while warm blood smothered his face. He knew Lisa had somehow been taken and he had been left behind.

But why? What had he done that was so wrong? He's never killed anyone or stole anything big.

Clueless to the answer, he mumbled painfully, "Lisa, Lisa." It drained all his energy. His head flopped over and slammed against the metal doorframe, knocking him unconscious. Brandon's dreams of happiness had vanished into the sky.

Chapter 12

The hardest part for Lisa was watching the sad look on Brandon's face. And the blood! How she wanted so badly to go back and help her lover, but she couldn't. She was powerless. A force was pulling her upwards that she couldn't resist, no matter how hard she tried.

Then her anxieties were unexpectedly allayed by a sense of comfort. Somehow she knew things would be perfect as they were meant to be, so she relaxed and was swept into paradise.

As she looked around, Lisa saw masses of people pouring into the Kingdom of God, all coming together in peace and harmony.

Families were reunited, old friends shaking hands, even pets were running to their beloved owner after years of separation. Lisa glanced outwards. Lush green pastures, mountains and sparkling waterfalls covered the environment. In the foreground a city of bright lights with skyscrapers that towered to the stars.

Lisa gasped in pleasure. There was something for everyone! In a nearby field lions were playing with sheep and dogs as though they belonged to one family.

She recalled that in heaven there was no killing, no racism, and no hatred: only peace and love between all. Adding to her surprise, Jesus floated down from the sky and appeared before everyone. Opening his arms in a warm greeting, he brought comfort to the masses. "Welcome, my children."

Lisa was fascinated. Jesus was standing directly in front of her, so close she could reach out to touch him. He stared into her eyes, which caused Lisa's heart to overflow with happiness.

Beside Lisa, a baby crawled on the ground towards him. Christ reached down, picked up the child and cuddled him in his arms. "You are such a pretty little thing. I love you."

The baby giggled as its eyes twinkled joyfully. Even the kids knew who this man was! Jesus handed the baby to its mother. "Take your child, Rosa."

Rosa stared in bewilderment. She took her child, mumbling, "You know my name."

"Of course I know your name, Rosa. I am the one who named you." Jesus spoke lovingly to the body of people, "It is my pleasure to give unto you the Kingdom of Heaven. For there are many mansions in my Father's house and I have prepared one for you. So rejoice evermore and be exceedingly glad, you are now in paradise."

Voices of cheer rang enthusiastically throughout the crowd. Jesus smiled, happy that this day had arrived. But there was much more to be done. He waved at the crowd and disappeared into the sky.

Chapter 13

As word of the disappearances spread, the earth had never seen such destruction. Havoc reigned supreme. Freeways were shut down. Wrecked cars covered the lanes. Fires swept uncontrollably through the cities. People mourned and cried for lost ones as others ran in fear.

Chaos swathed the streets worldwide.

Looters hit the stores hard, stealing everything that wasn't nailed down. Ramon, an older shopkeeper, stood behind his counter in the downtown district. Three kids were buying gum and then they disappeared. How could this be? There was no way they could've vanished like that.

Ramon knew they must be playing a game of hide and seek, so he decided to play with them. He stepped around the counter and shouted, "Boo." Sometimes the kids would sneak behind the shelves but this time they were nowhere.

A loud noise broke out at the front of the store. Ramon realized it had to be the kids and looked that way, except he saw an unexpected sight.

A dirty punk ran into the store swinging an enormous butcher knife wildly in the air.

Ramon had been robbed before and felt the safest behind his counter, so he jumped behind the wooden structure. But the thief ran straight at him, yelling, "Give me all your money, old man, or I'll slice you up like a fat pig."

The robber whipped the butcher knife in the air, slashing it back and forth in front of Ramon's face.

Terror devoured Ramon. "I don't have any money, I don't have any money. Please leave me alone," he begged. But the punk snarled at him, showing that the pleas had no effect.

Ramon was forced to defend himself and lunged for a pistol he kept under the cash register. Except the instant his fingers touched the handle, the thief sliced the butcher knife across his wrist that sliced his main artery.

Blood spewed from the wound, filling the air in streams of red.

The storekeeper screamed in horror but that aggravated the thief more. "Shut your stinking mouth!"

Ramon witnessed the true meaning of terror. He saw the butcher knife's shiny steel blade flash in the air just before it slashed his windpipe.

Ramon stepped backwards, coughing, as pain attacked his system. He tried to breathe but blood was filling his lungs, drowning him slowly. Blood spewed from his mouth and he dropped helplessly to the ground. Darkness began to cover his eyes.

With the spark of life fading, he willed his body into a final act of self-preservation. Ramon flinched his arm to push an alarm button that automatically closed and locked the doors, making exit nearly impossible.

The punk heard the doors lock. A siren blared and he knew he better get out before the cops arrived. He then saw a glimmer of life still abiding in the storekeeper. "You think you beat me, you piece of sorry trash. Take this and screw you." He flung his knife forcibly in the air.

Spinning head over heals, the cold steel of the butcher knife stabbed into Ramon's chest, piercing his heart that brought the final stage of death. His head flopped to the floor in a puddle of blood.

The thief laughed harshly at the dead man but he needed to find an escape route. Scanning the store, the easiest way came into view – the large plate glass window.

He ran at it and threw a hard kick, a kick that could surely burst any regular glass, but his foot bounced off like he had barely touched it. The window had to be safety glass. It would take something heavy to penetrate it.

A metal bubblegum rack was sitting nearby, so he grabbed it and hurled it at the window.

The rack smashed into it, shattering the glass into a thousand pieces, revealing a pathway to freedom.

The killer didn't waste a second as he rushed to the opening, but suddenly stopped. He hadn't taken any of the cash. Cursing himself, he ran back to the register and slammed his fist on the machine. It opened freely. After taking everything, even the pennies, he spit in Ramon's face. "You filthy old man, you said you didn't have any money. That's what you get for lying."

A police siren blared in the distance, telling him he better make his exit now. As he hurried to the opening, he noticed a small television on the counter and grabbed it.

Perhaps it was karma, perhaps not, but once he hopped through the busted window a jagged piece of glass ripped against his arm, cutting deeply into his flesh, causing him to drop the television. It smashed on the concrete into several pieces of broken glass and plastic.

The killer shook his arm in pain, slinging blood over the sidewalk. He yelled into the store, "This is all your fault, you old piece of crap. I'd kill you again if you weren't already dead!" The punk took off in anguish as blood flowed freely from his wound.

#   #   #

In a Houston, Texas subdivision, a woman ran down the street yelling, "Help! Aliens have taken everyone for food. They even stole my baby. Please help me!"

Glancing in every direction, she noticed a car driving her way. She waved her arms frantically as she ran to the center of the road to stop the vehicle. It worked, the car slowed to a halt. The driver rolled down his window cautiously.

Once the window was halfway open, she crammed her arms into the automobile and screamed, "Alien's have stolen my baby!"

Without a moment of hesitation, the driver slammed his foot on the gas pedal, leaving the potential harm behind. Smoke was streaming from his tires.

The woman stood helplessly in the middle of the street, crying. She fell to her knees while tears gushed down her face. Her baby was gone.

# # #

The streets were crowded in the heart of Manhattan. An older Bible thumper waved his book at the masses of confused people. "It's the beginning of God's judgments, that's what it is!"

A 1960's type hippie sat on a street curb smoking a joint. The Bible thumper ran to him, yelling, "Don't you know what's happening? It's all starting. The earth is going to burn in hell!"

Totally stoned out of his mind, the hippie didn't care either way. He was having a marvelous time getting high and that was all that mattered. He handed his joint to the loud person. "What's the matter, man? You're having a bad trip. Take a hit. It'll help you relax."

Jesus was hovering in the sky above the earth and could hear every word that was spoken. Christ shook his head in disappointment. There were so many rebellious and deceived souls sprinkled throughout the world. "And you wonder why you were left behind. Perhaps now, you should know that I am the Lord and shall reign forever. If you would have believed in my words and prophecies, then you shall have been saved from the coming tribulation. So be it, you chose."

In the twinkling of an eye, God sailed back to heaven.

The hippie was utterly awestruck. Somehow he heard every word that Jesus just stated and he interpreted that as a terrific sign. "Shoot man, this acid I took is far out. I'm already hearing voices. I think I'm about to take a ride!"

# # #

Los Angeles has been hit hard. Havoc ruled every neighborhood in the massive city. Ambulances raced down the streets prepared to help the injured. And it wasn't difficult to find someone in need. Automobiles littered the roads in every direction the eye could see.

An ambulance slid to a stop beside Lisa's car.

Two paramedics jumped out of the emergency vehicle and ran to the crashed auto, instantly spotting Brandon. He laid unconscious with his head tilted sideways. Dark blood coated his face.

"This one looks bad," the paramedic yelled as he tried to force the door open, but it was sealed shut by the accident. Metal crushed against metal. He instructed, "We need a crowbar."

His partner responded by cramming a curved bar into the door's jam. Yanking it with all his strength, he finally pried it open.

Brandon tumbled out. Right before he smashed onto the asphalt, the paramedic grabbed him. "Get the gurney, this one's bad. We have to get him to the hospital now!"

Chapter 14

Confusion abounded in every corner of Los Angeles' Cedars-Sinai hospital. Employees tried to cope with the excessive amounts of injured people being brought their way, but they were completely overwhelmed.

Adding to the disarray the staff had been cut drastically. Dozens of doctors, nurses and aids were swept up with the others, leaving the hospital in a total crisis.

A man ran down the hall covered in blood. "Help, help," he screamed. But the blood blinded his sight and he crashed into the wall, falling flat onto the floor. A nurse hurried to help him as paramedics pushed a gurney past her. "Get out of the way, coming through!" they yelled loudly.

Thankfully they were in a hurry because Brandon was the patient, and he looked dreadful.

Blood coated Brandon's body in a deathly red. His vision was a blur of images. His head throbbed so badly and a strong taste dominated his mouth, then he realized it was the taste of blood.

Was he dying?

The paramedics rushed him into the emergency room where a doctor and two nurses immediately jumped into action to help this young man. The doctor focused on the head wound as the nurses worked on his leg.

Brandon's blood pressure plummeted. The doctor shouted, "Give him fifteen milligrams of Demerol and patch the leg wound."

Brandon stared upwards in a daze. He could hear them speak but it was difficult to comprehend what they were saying, and then he felt a tingling sensation when a nurse pierced his arm with a syringe. Except the needle didn't bother him. The pain was minor compared to his other.

The shot made him dizzy, causing his vision to triple. His body became weaker by the heartbeat. But his mind still worked and it was focused on only one thing: the love of his life.

Brandon called out, "Lisa, Lisa!"

There was no response. But how could that be? Ever since they met Lisa had always been beside him. At that moment Brandon remembered what he saw, or what he thought he saw - Lisa disappearing in the sky with Jesus and thousands of others.

It had to be a dream, but he knew it wasn't. This meant Lisa was missing and he had to find her. Somehow, someway. And he was willing to give his life to accomplish the task.

As a burst of energy surged in his body, he shook his head to fight the medicine, but it was a losing battle. His body was shutting down along with his will to live.

Without Lisa, there would be no more love, no more happiness, and no more good times. So he had to make a last attempt to find her, even if it killed him.

Putting his heart and soul on the line, Brandon screamed, "Lisa, Lisa!"

His heart jolted and his body began to tremble, reaching unconsciousness. A nurse yelled, "Doctor, he's going into shock."

"Give him oxygen, now!" The physician pounded his fist on Brandon's chest. "Hand me the defibrillator."

The nurse handed him two paddles while the other nurse squirted a jelly substance on them. The doctor rubbed them together and placed them on his patient's bare chest, "Clear." An intense electrical charge engulfed Brandon's body that threw his chiseled chest high into the air.

Brandon came back to life. His eyes opened while a smile grew on his face like he was recalling a pleasant memory. But it was only temporary. His eyes closed as his body shut down. The doctor clenched the paddles. "Once again, clear!"

# # #

A few doors down the hallway from Brandon, Leroy and Maggie were watching television inside their hospital room. The program ended and the commercials begin to air. Maggie was sitting in a chair beside his bed and Leroy was frustrated. "Damn commercials, I hate all these commercials. They need to show more TV time than these commercials."

"What do you want me to do about it?" Maggie retorted sarcastically.

"I know what I want you to do about it. I want you to get me a cigarette."

"The hell you say! You're in a hospital bed, you can't smoke here."

"I don't care where I'm at. And why did I ever marry your lazy ass in the first place? Won't even get me a cigarette."

As they bickered, the news symbol flashed across the screen. "Channel Eight News Special Report." But nothing could stop Maggie from responding, "If you'd get a job then maybe I would hand you a cigarette."

"Shut up! I don't care to hear that crap, I want to hear this." Leroy focused on the television.

Paul, the newscaster, looked perplexed. "This is a special report. Inexplicable disappearances of people have happened worldwide. It's incredible. It's as if one third of the population has vanished. There have even been reported cases of gravesites blowing open with the dead bodies rising into the sky." Paul shook his head puzzlingly. "We have Tracy Sanders at the Shady Tree Meadows reporting live on this bewildering story."

#   #   #

A news crew adjusted their equipment to perfection. There was a lot of footage to be shot in the graveyard. History was in the making all around them. Mayhem encased every corner of the cemetery.

People were searching for loved ones while others stared in disbelief. Police investigated the scene as paramedics were helping those traumatized by the event.

The cameraman focused on an attractive female reporter.

"I'm Tracy Sanders at the Shady Tree Meadows Cemetery. This is by far the eeriest feeling I have ever experienced. Numerous

57

graves have been blown open from the inside out, and the scary part is the dead bodies that once occupied the caskets are gone. It's as though they disappeared into the air."

The cameraman scanned the shot over numerous open graves, and focused on one in particular: Mary Jo Williams. Panning to a close-up on the headstone, he swept the shot over the mound of dirt that surrounded the burial plot.

The casket was blown open and sat as clean as it was the day of construction.

Tracy yelled from behind the cameraman, "Alex, over here." He pointed the camera her way and spotted two paramedics pushing a stretcher twenty feet in the distance.

Tracy was quick on her feet. She dashed to the stretcher while talking over her shoulder, "It's been reported that this gentleman was present when it all took place. Let's see what he has to say."

Alex followed. He had to; her microphone cable was attached to his camera.

She finally slowed when she reached the stretcher. "Sir, I'm Tracy Sanders with Channel Eight news. It's been reported that you were present when this transpired. What happened?" Tracy shoved her microphone closer to Herman and finally got a glimpse of his face.

Herman's expression astonished her. He looked dead. His eyes were wide open like he had seen a ghost. But that didn't stop Tracy who was intent to get an award winning story, a story that could surely dominate the network news. "Sir, can you tell us what you saw?"

The paramedics bumped her with the metal cart to back her off. "Get out of the way. He can't talk to you, he had a heart attack."

"Is he dead?" Tracy shot back.

"No, not yet. So get out of the way," the paramedics demanded while they pushed the stretcher to the rear of the ambulance.

Tracy sighed as she spoke to the camera, "Paul, it is total confusion out here. No one seems to know what caused this desecration."

Paul stared solemnly into the camera. "Tracy, we have received numerous phone calls in the newsroom that this may have some type of Biblical implications. Have you heard any information similar to this?"

"Yes, I have. Just a few minutes ago a man was screaming that this was a sign from God. Then others claimed they actually saw Jesus Christ floating in the air!"

"It definitely looks like a scary situation out there. Thanks for the live report."

Except Tracy wasn't finished. "Paul, there's something I have to ask."

"Yes, Tracy?"

"If this does have some type of Biblical implications, then what's in store for us that were left behind?"

Paul's thoughts went cloudy. "Tracy, I don't care to think about that right now."

# # #

Leroy and Maggie's mouths dropped open. Leroy moaned from the depths of his gut, "Oh, my. What has happened?"

Maggie answered hesitantly, "I don't know, Leroy. But it don't look good."

"You don't think it's that Rapture crap those preachers on television were always talking about, do you?"

"I don't know, Leroy."

"Well, if it was, there's one good thing that can come from it."

"What's that? If you haven't noticed, we're still here," she complained.

"Don't you know what I'm talking about? Come on, woman, think with me here. We can finally settle that bet we have."

"What are you talking about, Leroy?"

"That bet we got about your mother. We can see if that piece of shit went to hell or not. Her grave will tell us!"

Maggie exploded. How dare he say ill tidings about her dear deceased mother? She grabbed the television remote and slung it at him. "You're a dirty piece of crap, that's what you are. You have no respect for the dead!"

59

Chapter 15

In the throne of God, John the Disciple was completely amazed by the events. He was witnessing the ending of the earth as we know it. The prophecy of the last days was in action.

Bolts of lightning blasted from the altar that made the area so bright John could see everything.

His gut feeling told him something awesome was about to occur, and he didn't have long to wait.

At that very second, the Spirit started to move fiercely in his golden chair that sent a wave of awareness throughout the environment. Then a large antique book containing seven seals appeared in his right hand.

Each seal was stamped firmly on the book binding it shut, and each seal was stamped with a number from one to seven.

John inquired of the angel that stood beside him, "Is that the book of the seven seals?"

"That is correct," the angel replied.

John could only wonder what the seven seals must stand for. Maybe it was because seven was God's number of perfection. The Holy Trinity was three sevens consecutive, 777.

Excited to discover the answer, John noticed more activity at the altar.

The Spirit held the book high in the air as a huge angel flew down from above and stated powerfully, "Who is worthy to open the book and loose the seals thereof?"

A silence overcame the throne. Nothing could be heard, not even a breath of air. The four beasts and twenty-four elders searched to see if anyone had been chosen.

John concluded that the book must be of major importance, but he couldn't understand why someone hadn't spoken. In these surroundings and around all of these influential beings, there had to be someone who could get the job done.

The disciple asked the angel, "What is taking place?"

"No one in heaven, nor upon earth, neither under the earth, was able to open the book or look thereon."

Tears formed in John's eyes. "Can we help?"

The angel noticed the tears. "Weep not, for one has been found worthy." He stretched his arms to the throne. "Behold, the Lamb of God!"

John stared at the altar in bewilderment. The area was buzzing with activity. The Spirit then shook the book forcibly and a lamb appeared in the middle of the throne.

Except the lamb had a distinctive appearance. Patches of its fur were covered in blood. It had clearly been stabbed in its side and blood was dripping to the ground.

Suddenly, a bright light flashed on the lamb that exposed its seven horns and seven eyes. John gawked at the creature. What kind of a lamb was this?

A starburst rippled in the sky and the lamb changed into the man, Jesus. Standing in front of the altar with blood dripping from his hands, feet and side, Jesus lifted his hands above his head and showed his wounds to everyone. He then closed his fists and crossed them over his chest. A moment later he uncrossed his arms and showed his palms.

The injuries were healed as though they were never scarred.

Reaching forward, Jesus took the book of the seven seals from the Great Spirit. Once he placed his right hand on the first seal, a smile grew on his face. It was time for man to see his true power!

Christ snapped the seal into smithereens.

At that exact moment, the clouds above parted as a white horse and rider flew down landing near the altar. Then, right beside them, another angel landed and they stared at each other in a disgusting fashion. Pure hatred dominated their eyes.

John became curious why they had such a scouring glare. "Why do they look at each other that way?"

"Wait, for you shall know shortly," his angel answered.

But John didn't have a clue. He then noticed something very bizarre about the horseman on the white horse.

The rider was a good-looking person who possessed an alluring aura. His right hand held a wicked bow and arrow, a tool obviously designed for destruction.

John had never seen a bow of this nature. Its shape and color was horrifyingly sinister, but yet it was quite appealing.

The angel standing beside the horse gave the rider a crown made of silver. The horseman grabbed it and threw it on his head as he yelled viciously at the altar, "This is not the last of me. You shall see me again!"

Instantaneously, the white horse took off into the air with a gust of wind surging behind him.

John's eyes showed confusion. The angel beside him inquired, "Don't you know what you have witnessed?"

"No, I don't have a clue! Please tell me," John pleaded.

"The breaking of the first seal is the final unleashing of the antichrist. He now has free reign over the world to dispense his destruction upon his people."

John was puzzled. "How can he be the evil one? The rider on the white horse is a good-looking person."

"That was then, this is now. The evil and sin that flows in his veins shall expose him shortly."

The antichrist raced through the sky, speeding from heaven to earth. John and the angel along with everyone in the throne could see the rider changing into his true appearance.

The force of the wind ripped away at the demon's skin, shredding the flesh off his face. His bloodshot eyes began to bulge while his body turned into a skeleton of burnt red skin.

Oozing blisters flourished over every inch of his torso covering him in slimy pus.

The antichrist's true inner being was revealed - pure evil, pure disgust, death. Screaming hysterically, the madness in his soul drove him crazy. His mission was to bring destruction worldwide.

I saw when the Lamb opened the first seal, and behold a white horse: and he that sat on him had a bow; and a crown was given unto him: and he went forth conquering, and to might conquer.
Revelation 6:1,2

Chapter 16

A strong breeze blew down a Washington D.C. street, picked up a pinecone and tossed it against the window of an elegant restaurant. Inside the establishment a group of four men were scrutinizing plans to keep the government running. They had to construct their statements carefully regarding the disappearances of citizens worldwide.

They must show everyone they were in full control of the situation.

A waitress approached the table. "Can I get you gentlemen anything else? Mr. Vice President, would you like something?"

Jeff Christensen smiled at her with a twinkle in his eye. "Yes you can, but I don't think it's on the menu." He grinned mischievously. He loved to play cat and mouse games with people, to treat them kindly and then do whatever he desired, and this waitress could be fun.

But for now he better stay focused on more important things: to keep the country stable and prosperous. "Another round of drinks will be sufficient."

"Yes sir, coming right away."

As she stepped away, Jeff stared at her impressive figure. "That girl has a fine looking ass."

One of his partners spoke, "Yep, I'd nibble on her like she was chewing tobacco." The others chuckled in agreement. Jeff glanced at the doorway and noticed an associate entering the building. The moment their eyes made contact, the associate headed to the bathroom.

Jeff stared closely at his colleagues. Not one of them had a clue to what was about to transpire, just oblivious to what the future had in store. Jeff stood. "Excuse me, gentlemen. I need to visit the restroom."

Once he stepped from the table, he accidentally bumped into the waitress. "I'm sorry, honey. I didn't see you. Are you okay?"

"Yes sir, Mr. Vice President. I'm all right. Just so you know, I'll welcome your bump anytime."

"Keep that thought in mind. Surprises can be fun."

She blushed from receiving this type of attention from such a powerful person. "Yes, sir. Your drinks will be waiting for you when you arrive at the table." She walked away.

Jeff could have pulled her back, but games could wait. Now was the time to write the future, to lay the foundation for his rise.

Heading to the restroom, he entered and stepped beside the associate who was washing his hands at the sink.

Jeff stared at his own reflection in the mirror, pleased with the image. He had strong handsome features, a dark tan, not a hair out of place and a two thousand dollar tailored suit.

The other man acknowledged, "Mr. Vice President, how are you tonight?"

"Shut up, I'm not here for small talk. Do you have everything planned?" he barked in a graveled voice.

The associate responded slightly sarcastically, "Have I ever failed you?"

"No, and you better not this time. And furthermore, if you ever, I mean ever, disrespect me with your sarcasm, I will personally slice out your tongue." Jeff stared piercingly at him for a few seconds, which probably seemed like an eternity to the other man, then reached into his pocket.

He threw a thick envelope on the countertop. "There's your money. Now get the job done and get it done quickly."

The associate flashed the cash in the fat envelope. "Yes sir, it's as good as finished."

# # #

In Los Angeles, Brandon arrived home from the hospital with his friend, Matt. Matt held the door open as Brandon hobbled in on a pair of crutches. He broke his leg in the accident and was having difficultly moving around.

Adding to his misery, his leg itched profusely inside the cast.

Matt tried to cheer him up. "Home, sweet home. How's it feel to be back, my friend?"

Still weak from the accident, Brandon sighed, "Anything is better than that hospital. A few days in that place could kill anyone." He plopped down on the couch and was ecstatic to be in his own domain.

Matt grabbed Brandon's overnight bag. "But look at you, you were tough enough to survive it. Where do you want this?"

Brandon pointed at a desk that housed his computer. "Just put it by the desk. And I should check my messages."

As Matt placed the overnight bag by the desk, Brandon dialed his cell phone and pushed the speaker button. "You have two messages. First message."

The first message was Brandon's Uncle who sounded very frenzied. "Brandon, hi, this is Uncle Joel. I'm not sure where to start. The past week has been extremely confusing and I need to speak to you about your parents. They have disappeared and I can't find them anywhere. Please give me a call. I hope you're doing well."

Brandon's expression went dead. "No, not my parents. Please don't let them be hurt." The machine continued, "Second message."

"Hello, Brandon. This is Philip from the office. I hope everything is all right. Would you give me a call when you receive this message? Thanks."

He pushed the off button and asked Matt, "I wonder what he wants?"

"I don't know. I told him about your accident so he's probably calling about that. I need to take off, you got everything situated?"

"Yeah, I'm okay. Thanks for the ride. I know it was asking a big favor with the roads tore up and cars crashed everywhere. What in the world is happening out there?"

"That's the million dollar question. I'm not sure, that's what I'm trying to figure out. You get better and talk with you later."

Brandon waved. "Thanks again, see you."

Matt left in a hurry. His mind was reeling from the occurrences of the past week. Four of his friends were swept up, yet he remained, and he was worried about what the future held in store.

When the door closed Brandon swaggered to the desk and sat. A tidal wave of emotions swallowed him. He was all-alone. His love, his life, had vanished into nowhere.

He rubbed his hand over the keyboard, wondering what he was going to do? Reaching down, he opened the top desk drawer. A velvet ring box sat inside with shiny gold lace tied around it.

Brandon just stared at it as a sharp pain attacked his heart. He grabbed the case, held it tightly, and then opened it. A large diamond ring glistened brilliantly, delivering sparkles of light. "At Parsay's, I was going to ask you to marry me."

Tears formed in his eyes. They dripped down his dry cheeks.

At the corner of the desk sat a picture of Lisa. Her face had such a happy smile, such a gorgeous smile. As if by instinct, he grabbed the photo and caressed it against his chest. He needed to hold her again. He had to. He missed her so badly.

Now the questions started to bombard him. How was he going to survive without Lisa? What happened to her? Where did she go? Why did she leave him behind? Couldn't she have grabbed his hand and taken him with her?

Brandon shook his head, it was too much to process. For now, he only wanted to think of how she made him feel so happy and complete.

Visions of their beautiful experiences impacted his thoughts, glimpses of pleasant times. The walks on the beach holding hands, watching the sun set behind the rugged mountains, and the time they spent in Hawaii making love in the warm ocean. They were even crowned the most loving couple on the island at an outdoor aloha barbecue, an honor that made Lisa feel spectacular.

Brandon smiled at the lovely experiences, and this helped him to regain some composure. So he placed the picture back on the desk and called the office. A receptionist finally answered after several rings, "Appleblum's Insurance, can I help you?"

"Hello Lucy, this is Brandon. It's great to hear you. How are you?"

It wasn't Lucy. "I'm not Lucy, she no longer works here."

"What do you mean? What happened to her?"

"Look, I'm very busy. I don't have time for your questions. What do you want?"

"What! Connect me to Philip Appleblum."

"Who's calling?" she snapped back.

"Brandon Summers. That's who's calling!" The receptionist transferred the call. Brandon spoke lightly, "That girl's rude. I'm going to hate working with her."

Philip answered in a caring way, "Hello, Brandon. How are you?"

He calmed down after hearing Philip. "A lot better, sir, thanks for asking. How are things at the office?"

Philip's voice changed from friendship to a professional tone. "Brandon, I know you just got out of the hospital so this may not be the best time to talk. Would you like to call me back later?"

Brandon grasped that something was up, and he hated to play games. He asked bluntly, "Philip, if there's a problem let's cut to the chase. We've known each other for too long. Am I being fired?"

"Not fired, but laid off," Philip replied. "I don't know if you're aware of this but approximately forty percent of the population has vanished. And with the extreme amount of claims being filed the insurance industry is collapsing worldwide. I hate to do this but I have to let you go."

"Aw, man. This isn't right. What about Matt?"

"I'm going to keep Matt around for a while longer. He also does a lot of the administrative work and you were always straight sales. I do wish you the best of luck and I'll have a courier drop off your final check with some severance pay. Fair enough?"

"Whatever," Brandon stated downheartedly. What else could he say? He hung up the phone and stared blankly at nothing. "First, my woman, then my parents, and now my job. What's next?"

Chapter 17

The sun's light beamed forcibly through Joyce's windshield directly into her eyes. She quickly put her hand above her face to block the rays, but it was useless. It couldn't help her to see the road any better. Tears obstructed her view far worse than the sun ever could. Ever since Janie, her three-year-old baby and the love of her life, disappeared a few days ago nothing had been the same.

How did it happen? Her little Janie was giggling like a happy baby when she vanished out of her arms and disappeared out of sight.

Just the thought of her missing child destroyed her heart, making tears drip down her smooth dark skin.

Joyce shook her head to toss them from her cheeks, but the tears kept flowing. There was no stop, so she exited the freeway at the next off ramp and pulled her car to the side of the road.

Joyce had to regain her senses. She had too, somehow, someway.

As she reached forward to turn off the engine, she wished she could turn off the pain that throbbed in her heart.

Joyce recalled a past memory when the doctor handed Janie to her for the first time and how complete of a woman she felt. "My sweet little baby," she whispered as she held her so softly, so lovingly.

Smiling at the pleasant thought, Joyce looked in her purse for a napkin but her eyes were pulled to a picture of Janie. That was all it took. Tears flowed again like water rushing down a river.

How was she going to bear the workday?

This was the first day back since it took place and the past few days have been pure hell. But Joyce knew she must stay strong.

She glanced in the rearview mirror. Her own reflection was staring back, an image of a strikingly attractive black woman. Except it also showed the image of a terribly confused person.

Joyce remembered that a friend had mentioned the talk radio shows, so she turned on the radio and dialed in a station. The current caller was asking the all-important question. "Why did her son disappear and why was she still here?"

Joyce held her breath. The radio captured her attention and she was desperate to know the answer. The woman caller started with a raspy tone by mentioning her son had a teacher in school who occasionally talked about God. She broke down sobbing, confessing she would always tell her boy that God was fictional. But her son consistently sided with the teacher. By now, the caller was crying aloud. "What took my son from me?"

"Well, ma'am, I don't have an answer for that question. But our special guest in the station could possibly help," the talk show host admitted. "Callers, I would like to welcome a friend of mine, father Johnson from the First Saints Church."

"Thank you for the introduction, Larry. But please, do not refer to me as 'father' any longer. Since I was left behind, I have studied the Scriptures with all my heart. And there is a verse that literally stunned me. It's in the twenty-third chapter, verse nine, of Matthew. It's when Jesus was rebuking the Pharisees for being hypocrites, and he told his followers, "Call no man your father upon the earth: for one is your Father, which is in heaven.""

Larry tilted his head. "You're a priest of a church, I thought I was supposed to call you father."

"I used to be of the same mind, Larry, and I was taught the same. But it's not the truth. What Christ clearly taught is that you should never call any man your father in a spiritual sense. Of course this verse has no bearing to calling your parent, father. It means you should never call a person 'father' in a spiritual sense. So now I don't like anyone to call me father. It is not correct in God's word, and it is pure blasphemy."

"Thanks for the clarification. That is very interesting! Now let's try to help this caller with her question."

"Hello, miss. Concerning your question, there is truth to what your son stood for," Mr. Johnson confirmed.

"How can it be true? If it is true, then why were you left behind? If you have the title of 'father' in a church, why are you still here?" the caller asked hesitantly.

"That's a great question," Mr. Johnson admitted. "You see, in my church, I never taught the doctrine in Revelation. To answer your question more simply, I never believed in it myself."

"But if you're a preacher of some sort and if the Bible teaches it, then how could you not believe in it?"

"Believe me, ma'am, I have asked myself that very question every second since this transpired. I made a terrible mistake. And please give me the chance to say one thing to my congregation. I am so sorry, please forgive me."

As the words left his lips silence dominated the airwaves. The caller spoke first, "I can tell that you feel sorry for your mistake. I hope you'll be forgiven. May I ask one more question?"

"You can ask anything," he replied sincerely. The woman pleaded, "Is there anyway I can be with my child again?"

"Yes, there is. Please listen to these words very carefully. Jesus is your only way to be with your loved ones again. You must truly give your life to the Lord and believe that he is the only way to enter heaven. As the Bible clearly states, 'No person can come unto God, except by Christ.'"

"I am so bewildered," the caller cried. "How do I do what you say?"

"It's easy. Just pray to Jesus and ask him to come into your heart and save your soul. He already knows you want to be with your child, so humble yourself and ask him to help guide you. To change you from your sinful ways and to do the right thing. And read the Bible."

"I'll do it and I'll do it right now. Thank you so much." The lady caller hung up.

Joyce sat spellbound.

She turned off the radio, looked to heaven and prayed with all her heart, "God, I know I haven't been the best person I could have. But please let me be with my baby again. I believe you are the only Son of God. Please forgive me of my sins and save my soul so I can be with you and my child."

A feeling of peace shrouded her spirit; a sensation of pleasure blanketed her in warmth. Joyce knew that one day she would hold her Janie again. She smiled at her daughter's picture. "I will see you again, my little baby. I love you so much."

She kissed the photo, placed it back in her purse and drove up the freeway ramp.

A work crew was standing in the middle of the onramp pulling a wrecked or abandoned automobile out of a ditch. Joyce concluded the driver of the auto must have vanished like the others. Why else would somebody leave such a nice car behind? The workers pulled the vehicle out of the ditch and waved her by. She sped up to get on the freeway.

# # #

Energy was building in the throne. John was surprised as he saw a shiny ball sailing through the air. It bounced around and then smashed into the book of the seven seals that Jesus held, and Christ snapped the second seal into dust.

John stood spellbound. Everything was happening so rapidly. He looked at the angel beside him and began to pray.

The angel told him forcibly, "Pray not to me. You pray only to Jesus Christ and to no one else. And I mean to no one else!"

John shuddered at the words, and then something occurred at the altar that stole his attention. The second horseman appeared on a fiery red horse along with another angel that held a huge sword. The angel handed the sword to the horseman.

The rider grabbed the sword and held it high. Pure evil was pumping through his veins as he flew to the earth waving the sword wildly.

When he had opened the second seal, there went out another horse that was red: and power was given unto the rider to take peace from the earth, and that they should kill one another: and there was given unto him a great sword.
Revelation 6:3,4

# # #

A skinhead was speeding down the freeway in his beat-up pickup truck. "Yee-haw, I just got me the urge to kill a nigger!"

It was early morning - the best time for a cold beer. He grabbed a can from the passenger's seat but opened it too quickly, which sprayed beer all over his shirt. "Shit, I hate when it splashes on me. I guess that means I need to drink it up." He drank the entire beverage in one massive gulp, burped loudly, then crushed the can and threw it on the floorboard. "That's all I needed. Now it's time to find someone to screw with."

It didn't take long to find his target. His eyes were quick to spot an attractive black woman, Joyce. The racist swerved his beat-up pickup truck toward Joyce's car, almost ramming into it.

Joyce's instinct forced her to pull out of the way, barely avoiding an accident. His truck came inches from her door, so she rolled down her window and yelled, "Hey, watch where you're going. Be careful."

The punk laughed, loving the fact he had startled her. His chrome-covered pistol sat on the passenger's seat and without hesitation, he aimed the hardened steel 6-shooter at her face and pulled the trigger four times.

Gunshots exploded as fireballs flashed in the cockpit of his vehicle. "Screw you, bitch! Die," he screamed in pure hatred.

The first bullet smacked Joyce in the head, splattering her brains throughout her car. Splotches of blood covered the leather interior while tissue fragments dripped off the rearview mirror.

Joyce's body was tossed over the console which whipped the steering wheel to the side, causing her automobile to zip off the road. It crashed into a steep embankment exploding into a huge fireball.

Once the skinhead saw the car ignite into flames, he burst out laughing. "That's one down and millions more to go!" A smile crossed his face as he proceeded down the freeway, proud of his performance.

Though Joyce's body lay dead in a ditch, her spirit was on a trip to paradise to be with her beautiful child once again.

This time they'll spend an eternity of peace and love, a Godly binding that could never be broken.

Chapter 18

Brandon sat at his kitchen table reading a magazine. The relaxation time felt incredible, but his stomach growled like it was saying feed me and feed me now. He glanced at his belly and was glad to have an appetite.

Ever since Lisa disappeared, or whatever happened, food had basically become last on his list of importance, and he had lost several pounds because of it. Except he knew he must eat to give his body nutrition.

Bottom line, he had to eat or he would die. So he decided to visit his local diner.

Jumping to his feet, Brandon headed to the doorway and instinctively tapped his back pocket to make sure his wallet was there. Unfortunately, it was MIA. "Oh, no. Where did I leave my wallet?" He immediately rehashed every step he took since arriving home last night, and his bedroom became first on the list.

Without hesitation, he rushed down the hallway but accidentally tripped over a pile of dirty clothes that littered the floor. Brandon fell face first, smacking his chin on the floor.

"Darn," he yelled as he stared at the pile of dirty clothes. "I guess it's time to do laundry." After rubbing his hairy chin, he realized it was also time for a shave.

Brandon knew he had several chores to catch up on, except Lisa consumed his thoughts. But somehow he had to move on, to devote some time to himself.

Brandon laughed. That "devoting time to yourself" crap sure sounded terrific, except it was a tough task to accomplish. So he better deal with the present and find his wallet.

Entering his bedroom, he stepped into a complete mess. Clothes were scattered everywhere, equaling another chore to add on the list.

He then noticed his wallet sitting in plain view on the dresser. A picture of Lisa was just inches away.

His sight was pulled to the picture like a magnet pulling a hunk of steal. Once he stared at it, his heart plummeted to his stomach. It had become so difficult to look at her picture.

In the beginning it was different, he still had hope that she was coming home and this would be a bad dream.

But this wasn't a dream. This was reality. Lisa was gone, and he was all-alone.

Unfortunately, that wasn't his only problem. The confusion he endured daily had become pure chaos. He didn't know what to do, where to go, whom to see or who to trust.

Brandon shook his head. He had to dismiss these thoughts and he had to dismiss them now before they drained the life from his soul.

Except the main question still loomed, "What in the world was going on, and how did he get sucked into the middle of it?"

Since he didn't have an answer, he put the wallet in his rear pocket and stared at himself in the dresser's mirror.

The sight wasn't pleasing. Wrinkled clothes, unshaven face, and bags were beginning to show underneath his eyes. He decided that once he returned home a long hot shower, a close shave, and a good night sleep would be the perfect remedy.

#   #   #

Encircling the throne of God, a shimmering rainbow was glowing brightly. John found everything to be absolutely fascinating. The spontaneity of being here was pure excitement. Surprises abounded at every turn.

As he wondered what could be next, several bolts of lightning blasted from the altar. The intense sound nearly burst his eardrums. Then a gigantic angel sailed past him that caused a strong wind to whip across John's body.

The angel flew toward the throne and proclaimed, "The time is at hand to bring famine and inflation upon the world."

"So be it, let it be done," the Spirit's voice in the golden chair rumbled.

74

Jesus nodded at the new angel as he crumbled the third seal.

At that instant, a solid black horse with a horseman appeared from nowhere. The horse reared his body upwards and started swinging his hoofs like a prizefighting boxer.

The horseman on the wild beast held a pair of balancing scales high above his head and laughed venomously.

The angel ordered, "Go." The horseman screamed at the throne as he flew away holding the scales.

When he had opened the third seal, and lo, I beheld a black horse; and he that sat on him held a pair of balances. And power was given unto him to place inflation upon the earth.
Revelation 6:5,6

Chapter 19

Cruising down the street, Brandon was staring at the palm trees that lined the road. He loved the outdoors. The smell of nature always brought him happiness, and he was feeling good today. Within a couple minutes, he arrived at his neighborhood grocery store, the Value Save, and parked in a space near the front. But once he got out of his car, his luck changed. He accidentally stepped into a wad of gum, and the heat of the day melted the gum that made it stick firmly to the bottom of his shoe.

"Oh, man. This sucks," Brandon mumbled as he headed to the store. Each time he stepped, his shoe would stick to the pavement, so he began to scrap it across the asphalt.

A lady standing near the doorway stared at him, puzzled to what he was doing. His body was bent over scrapping his foot like a hunchback.

Brandon noticed her but didn't pay any mind. He finished removing the gum, approached the doorway and joked, "I'm an actor practicing for a jungle movie. How'd you like my monkey impression?"

She looked at him with wide eyes. "That was a great monkey impression. I thought you looked like King Kong the way you moved. You should get that acting job easily."

"Well, thank you, ma'am. I appreciate the vote of confidence," he stated politely, and then noticed an advertisement sign posted by the entranceway. The sign's contents were shocking.

Top Label Whiskey – pint size – regular $22.00,
Today's Special $18.00.
Cigarettes – per pack – regular $10.50,

Today's Special $9.00.

"What!" Brandon shrieked. "That's no special." But the soaring prices weren't only at this establishment. They have been skyrocketing at every location and from every type of retailer. Even the ninety-nine cent hamburgers at the fast food places were now two dollars and ninety-nine cents, not to mention the escalating gasoline prices that were too expensive for anyone to afford.

It was robbery but what could a person do? They had to eat and drive, so they were forced to pay the exorbitant fees.

Brandon heard his stomach roar. He didn't care what the sign said – he wanted some food!

Entering the store, he grabbed a carrying basket and proceeded down the first aisle, the cooler section.

Several displays of beer were stacked in the large open-air freezers, beverages from every country in the world. And it didn't take long to find his favorite. Their popular blue label was easy to spot. He picked up a cold six-pack, placed it in his basket and then noticed the price sticker.

It basically stunned him. "Twelve dollars for a six pack!"

Brandon quickly scanned the cost of the other beers. It was startling. The prices varied from eleven dollars for the cheapest to twenty-five dollars for the imported, and he compared the other domestics to his selection. "Hey, check it out. They cost more than mine. That's smart to keep their prices down for the average working man."

Happy with finding the best deal in these rough times, Brandon headed to the meat department. The more he thought about a thick steak the more his mouth began to drool. That would be exactly what the belly doctor ordered. He saw the steaks. But before he just grabbed one, he decided to look closer at the price sticker. So he focused on the label.

Instantaneously, his dream of a juicy steak vanished like a puff of smoke. "Nineteen dollars for a little steak!" he shrieked. "That's a rip-off."

In Washington D.C., the sun blazed in the sky. The President of the United States was jogging down the street with several security agents surrounding him, protecting him from any estranged persons.

The President glanced at the blue sky. "This is such a gorgeous day. It's hard to believe what has happened."

"Yes sir, Mr. President. It sure is," Raymond, his advisor, responded.

The President went into thought and then asked Raymond, "Do you have an answer for the recent tragedies? It has almost shut the government down and has taken the world by surprise. Think of how many taxpayers and voters we lost."

"No, sir. I wish I did have an answer."

"Yeah, I understand. At least jogging relieves some of the stress," the President joked, trying to find some humor.

"Yes, sir. It sure does," Raymond agreed.

There was another question that haunted the President, one that really bothered him. He mumbled lightly, "But why was I left behind?"

Continuing his jog, the President believed the worst was over. Except fate had more in store.

A loud gunshot shattered the calmness. Soaring at lethal speed, a bullet smacked the President dead center in his chest, ripping his upper torso apart. Pieces of flesh littered the air as blood splattered like it was raining red.

The force of the impact threw him backwards several feet. He landed brutally on the ground, flopping like a leaf in a windstorm.

The President grabbed his chest while blood gushed profusely from his mouth. He pleaded, "Help me. Help me," and coughed up a spring of blood high into the air.

"Oh, no!" Raymond yelled. He noticed that the President was trying to speak. He had to hear every word his boss said, that was his job, his duty. Raymond put his head near the President's mouth, but he should have looked first.

A puddle of blood splashed across his face, swallowing him in a deathly red. Both his eyes and ears were covered, leaving him deaf and blind. His natural senses had vanished.

A void of blackness shrouded Raymond, but he knew what had to be done.

Raymond shook his head from side to side, trying desperately to restore his vision, then wiped his shirtsleeve over his eyes. This restored his sight.

In the same motion, he yanked his pistol from its holster and jumped to his feet, waving the weapon in every direction. His eyes and pistol worked as one as he scanned every inch of his surroundings. He had to hunt down the cold-blooded sniper.

Raymond's worst nightmare was happening at his feet – his general was dying and he was powerless. Well, perhaps not powerless: he could kill the sons-a-bitch that did this. As blood dripped down his face, he didn't pay it any attention.

He focused on every tree, every building, and behind every rock.

Unfortunately, nothing was there but shadows lurking in his mind. "Where did it come from?" he screamed hysterically.

No one answered. The other agents were just as busy surrounding the President's body. The attack happened too fast. A quick hit and run. The worst kind.

"Damn!" Raymond hissed. He knew the sniper had already fled to freedom. This meant a swift capture of the killer was vanishing with every second.

#   #   #

Down the hallway from Brandon's old hospital room, Leroy and Maggie were bickering. "I can't believe we're still stuck in this hospital. And there's too many commercials on tonight," Leroy grumbled crustily.

"If you'd quit drinking so much and get a job then your liver would be better and we wouldn't be stuck here."

"Shut up, Maggie! The TV's back on. I want to hear it!"

Maggie didn't care what he said. She was too busy clipping her toenails and that was far more important than that old windbag. The problem was, she hadn't clipped them in a while and was having trouble. Squeezing the clippers with all her might, her body started to tremble. But her big toenail wouldn't cut.

79

So she pretended it was Leroy's head.

Once that visual entertained her thoughts, Maggie squeezed the clippers so hard the toenail snapped off and flew at the speed of a projectile.

It smacked Leroy on the side of his face.

"What the hell are you doing over there?" he screeched. "What did you throw at me? I better not be bleeding."

"I'm sorry, my toenail must have gotten you."

"A toe nail!" Leroy bitched while massaging the injured area. "What are you talking about? That won't a toenail, that was a missile! Them sorry terrorists ain't got missiles that powerful."

"I can't help it, they're hard to clip."

"They wouldn't be so hard if you'd cut'em more than once a year." Leroy rubbed the side of his face, whining in fear, "I think you drew some blood." The moment he realized there wasn't any, he became cockier. "You got lucky, woman. There ain't no blood. Because if there was..."

Maggie stopped him mid-sentence. "Shut up, I don't care to hear it! The thing about the President is coming on."

Leroy glanced at her and burped. "There you go. That's what I think about them filthy politicians. They're just a bunch of crooks so I don't care what happens to them."

Maggie was about to yell but the TV announced, "This is a Channel Eight News break."

The newscaster appeared with two political reporters. As the Vice President, Jeff Christensen, was preparing to be sworn in as President, the political reporters talked about the upcoming events. "Tom, with the horrible assassination of the President, Vice President Christensen is quickly being sworn in as President to calm the country. Do you think this strategy will work?"

Maggie didn't wait for the reporter's response. She turned down the volume with a look of sadness covering her face. "I can't believe the President was assassinated. It's such a tragedy."

"Who cares, I never liked that damn President anyway!" Leroy responded grumpily.

Chapter 20

Dry hot winds blew swiftly through the dusty plains of an African village. A large gust picked up a piece of briar bush and threw it against the head of an elderly native woman. Zoolu immediately covered her face to avoid being injured, and then she thought of the most important thing in her life: her twelve-year-old grandbaby.

Just before she panicked of the child's whereabouts, she spotted the kid sitting safely by their hut.

Ever since the girl's mother died of AIDS, the precious child had become the center of her universe.

But when Zoolu saw her, her eyes didn't radiate the sparkle that most grandmothers would have. Her hopes appeared to be diminishing. Her heart broke every time she stared at the child.

The girl had become so skinny and undernourished.

Zoolu felt sorrow. She knew she was only an old lady that was about to starve herself, which made her heart sink even further. But there was nothing more she could do. She already gave the child one-half of her food every night. Zoolu looked at the faces of the small group of villagers that she worked beside.

Each one had the same expression: heartache, hunger, despair. Hopelessness flourished around her.

Zoolu recalled a time when a missionary crew came into their village with medicine and strange food products. And it wasn't the items or the preaching about God that stayed with her; even her granddaughter didn't care to hear it. It was a story about some type of box they called a television that showed moving pictures of the world.

She wondered if her country had ever been shown on a picture box? Did it show how unlivable this place really was? If so, why

81

hasn't someone helped? Zoolu stared at the ground just as a growling noise echoed in the distance.

# # #

In the throne, the Spirit rumbled in his golden chair. Fireballs flickered above the altar producing massive light. John blurted, "Wow, that was something!"

The angel beside him laughed. "Just wait, you haven't seen anything yet."

John loved the response. He could only imagine what would be next, and didn't have long to wait.

A voice thundered from the altar, "The time is at hand for the next judgment."

The fourth seal was snapped and a pale colored horse with a rider appeared from nowhere. The horseman's eyes glowed in a hideous red as he growled satanically at the throne. Then the horse and rider took off into the air, ready to dispense terror upon the earth.

When he had opened the fourth seal, I looked, and behold a pale horse: and his name that sat on him was Death, and hell followed with him. And power was given unto him over the fourth part of the earth, to kill with sword, and with hunger, and with the wild beast of the earth.
Revelation 6:7,8

# # #

Zoolu was hard at work in the African village. An elderly man sitting close to her smacked his grain crushing stick on the ground. "I'm tired of crushing this grain every day."

Zoolu stated softly, "We all hate to crush the grain but there's nothing else to eat." She mechanically rolled her stick in the pan of oats. "If we don't work together, how can we survive?"

Her words reached his heart or perhaps his stomach, whichever he proceeded to roll his stick in the pan. "I'll crush this stuff but I don't have to like it."

She understood. It took hours of work to produce only a tiny morsel of edible grain. At that moment another strange noise reverberated from behind.

Zoolu twisted around to search for the odd sound, except it seemed to be generating from several different areas. A gust of wind blew that tore several sticks from a hut's roof. They crashed onto the ground in a puff of dust.

Once Zoolu witnessed this, she concluded they must be the culprit of the noise. Sticks always fell from the mud huts so she continued with her grain crushing.

In the bush trail thirty feet from the group, a pack of lions were stalking the villagers, waiting. The leader, an extremely large lion, licked his corrosive tongue over his famished teeth. Drool dripped from his mouth and splashed on the ground.

The lion roared loudly, leapt from behind the bushes and charged the people. His entire pack followed directly behind.

The old man near Zoolu was the closest to the herd of charging beasts, and was their first victim. Four lions jumped on him and sunk their teeth into his flesh, tearing at his body. One animal whipped his arm back and forth so forceful it ripped the limb from his torso.

The old man screamed in terror. His blood was gushing as another lion sank its teeth deeply into his side, shredding the intestines from his stomach. His guts flopped on the dirty ground that splashed blood onto the lion's face.

The beast threw his head back, growling ferociously, loving the taste of fresh meat.

Blood splattered across Zoolu's face as she stared in pure terror. But another thought dominated over everything else.

Where was her grandbaby?

Thankfully she saw the child unharmed outside of their hut. Zoolu yelled with everything she had, "The hole, the hole."

The instant the child heard the instruction and noticed the attacking beasts, she ran for the hole, or their hiding place, as quickly as her little feet would carry her.

Zoolu watched the love of her life enter the stick hut, and then heard a loud growling sound from behind. The native woman turned to stare at what would be sure death.

The bloodshot eyes of the male lion were piercing at her.

Zoolu knew that whatever she would endure, whatever pain she might experience, it couldn't compare to the anguish of her grandbaby being hurt.

And there was only one way she knew of to help save the sweet child.

With no concern for herself, Zoolu jumped to her feet and waved her arms hysterically. She screamed at the top of her lungs, "You'll take me before you can have her!" The native woman ran at the lion in full force and hopped on his back, but her strength was nothing compared to his.

The instant she landed on the beast, the lion thrashed from side to side, throwing Zoolu to the dirt.

She slammed on the ground, knocking her breathless. Zoolu gasped for oxygen while trying to catch her breath, except her torment wasn't near its end.

The lion dove through the air centering his focus on Zoolu's neck. The beast bit hard, sinking his teeth into her flesh, and ripped Zoolu's throat from her body.

The villagers screamed helplessly from being eaten alive. Their blood and body parts were flung everywhere, littering the ground in bright red.

As the wild beasts savaged this community, the child hid safely in the hole, traumatized.

Chapter 21

Consumed with a slight fear of his financial future, Brandon drove down the street to the unemployment office. It was time to pick up his final check. The benefits had expired and this produced a strong dilemma.

How was he going to survive without any money entering the household?

He had been looking for a job but finding employment was tricky. The world wasn't as it was. The job market had basically plummeted to zilch.

A stoplight at the corner of the street turned red. Brandon slowed to a stop at the intersection with caution.

In this new world, his instinct always forced him to verify the coast was clear. While glancing around, he noticed a homeless man begging for money at the side of the street.

Ever since the Rapture, or whatever it was that happened, many more people have been living in the streets. The disappearances left millions of households without a money earner or no way to support their family, which eventually put them in the streets.

Though it had been some time since it occurred, havoc still reined worldwide.

The homeless man held out his hands asking two approaching teenagers for spare change or something to eat. One kid yelled, "I have something for you to eat. How about a knuckle sandwich?" The hoodlum punched the homeless man in the nose, knocking him to the ground. Then they beat him mercilessly.

The first kid smacked him several times as the other kicked him in the side, causing the homeless man to gasp painfully.

Then the two punks laughed out loud and ran away leaving the beaten man defenseless on the sidewalk, curled in a fetal position like a small child.

Brandon couldn't believe what happened. But what could he do?

If he went to help he would have to leave his car in the middle of the intersection, and he'd probably get shot. Brandon sighed deeply, "Oh man, these streets are getting mean. There has to be an answer."

#   #   #

In the Throne of God, commotion was stirring near the altar. John's curiosity peaked. "What shall happen next?"

The angel beside him spoke of knowledge, "Just wait, this should be interesting."

The moment John heard that, his anxiety rose – will this judgment be entirely different? Now an immense feeling of anticipation swept through the surroundings as the crystal lake in front of the altar began to bubble. Ripples were bursting through its calm demeanor and then it turned into a sea of souls.

Jesus stood at the right side of the mighty Spirit. "Now is the time to see." He snapped the fifth seal on the antique book and the sea of souls screamed for their killers to be avenged.

The Spirit flowed in his exquisite chair from hearing the pleas of his children whom had died for his testimony. He waved his arm over the crystal lake.

John was amazed. Every soul in the crystal lake was suddenly clothed in a pure white robe like they were being born into new.

God charged, "For you shall rest for a short season, until your fellow servants and brethren should be killed as you were for my testimony." Bolts of lightning exploded in the sky.

John's eyes surged in size while he stared in pure awe.

When he had opened the fifth seal, I saw under the altar the souls of them that were slain for the word of God, and for the testimony which they held: And they cried with a loud voice, saying, How

long, O Lord, holy and true, until you judge and avenge our blood
on them that dwell on the earth?
Revelation 6:9,10

Chapter 22

Several people hurried into the lobby of a large church to attend the early service, but the place was filling too quickly. The ushers were already struggling to find the newcomers a seat. This might even come as a surprise considering this was the largest church on the East Coast of the United States.

Immediately following the disappearances, church burnings swept through the country and basically the world.

Churches and synagogues were burnt into flames from the smallest cities to the major metropolitan areas, and this made it difficult to find a place to congregate. For several months the dominating news was about citizens literally giving their lives to protect their houses of worship.

People everywhere were searching for something, anything, to believe in. Masses were convinced that an unusual phenomenon was in action. A lot of folks have also come forth and publicly accepted God as their savior.

The local newspaper printed a couple articles of interest. The first was an interview with several scholars who said the massive amount of church burnings were a direct result of the first seal judgment, the final unleashing of the antichrist.

The other article had a picture of seven people standing on top of a church with guns in hand, fighting off a gang of kids who were trying to catch the building on fire. The photo resembled the catastrophes of the Los Angeles riots in many ways.

Since most of the churches have been destroyed, the government subsidized a program that built enormous sized buildings for the purpose of worship.

People flocked through the doors, crowding the lobby. The ushers were now forced to turn them away. The place was completely full, standing room and all.

Even though faith seekers packed the building, an unusual feeling encased the establishment. There wasn't a Cross or anything related to Jesus inside the structure.

Standing behind a pulpit talking to the congregation, father Jack Smitty was dressed in a Catholic priest robe with his salt and pepper hair styled to perfection.

He moved from the pulpit while speaking to the congregation in a heartening tone, "It's true that I'm a priest, and the main reason why God left me behind is to help guide his flock during this rough time. I know things may seem difficult, but there is some good news of hope and change. And that good news is Jeff Christensen, our President of the United States! He is one of us. He speaks the truth. So please listen to what he has to say. He can help us through this nightmare."

Smitty stopped to stare over the masses of people. His plan was finally in action.

# # #

Sitting alone in his apartment, Brandon was rehashing the good old times. For several months he has been coping with Lisa's disappearance, but recently things had been complex. Reality had set in that he'll probably never see his lover again, to touch her skin or smell her radiant fragrance.

Consumed in how things could have been, visions of the life they would've shared bounced in his head. The love they could've experienced. He shook his head in the attempts to clear his thoughts.

A slight depression has attacked him. It was mainly because Lisa was taken from him. She didn't leave him or breakup with him, and he didn't have any say or control over the situation.

He was powerless with no way to protect her.

Brandon's heart longed but he knew he better find something to overpower these emotions, and he better find it before they destroyed him.

His old friend Matt popped into mind. He grabbed the telephone, recalling the number from memory. Matt answered after two rings, "Hello."

"Matt, it's Brandon. Long time no hear. How are you?"

"Brandon, what's happening? I haven't seen you in a while. Where have you been?" Matt responded cheerfully.

"I'm sorry, I've just been hanging. Thought I'd call to see how things are going."

"Things are okay and it's great to hear your voice, except you sound a little down."

"Yeah, I was thinking about Lisa. Things are so different now. I sure miss the old days."

"I know what you mean. It's amazing at how the world has changed. But let's talk about that later, you caught me in the middle of grilling hamburgers. Why don't you come over for a bite to eat?"

Matt's words astonished Brandon. They were music to his ears. Even the rock-n-roll voice of Elvis couldn't make music this beautiful. Nothing could beat a big fat juicy hamburger. "What!" he responded enthusiastically. "You actually have real hamburgers. Shoot man, you don't have to ask me twice. I'll be there in a few!"

Matt chuckled. "Okay, buddy, but you better get here quickly before I eat it all up. See you soon."

Brandon didn't waste a moment. He leapt from the couch, grabbed his jacket and bolted out the door. He was on a mission and it was going to be a tasty one. The kind he enjoyed the most: a food mission!

Chapter 23

Brandon's foot was placed firmly on the gas pedal. It was pedal to the metal time! Speeding down the road, he wondered which had more influence – seeing his old friend Matt again or sinking his teeth into a juicy hamburger.

The answer was irrelevant; they both would be terrific.

As Brandon turned down Matt's street, a pleasant memory impacted his thoughts. It was a time when Matt had asked him to housesit for the weekend, and it was a warm evening - all he needed to persuade Lisa into going skinny-dipping. Brandon tossed her into Matt's small swimming pool and dove in behind, splashing water over the concrete edges. Then they ripped off each other's bathing suits in seconds flat. Just recalling that filled his heart with happiness.

Brandon parked in front of the house. While stepping to the front door, he cleared his mind of past memories and rang the bell.

Within seconds, Matt answered the door with a large smile on his face. "Brandon, it's great to see you, buddy!"

"Hey, thanks Matt. I'm sorry it's been a while but you know how things are."

"Don't even think about it. Come on in, I'm glad you're here. And I hope you're hungry because I just finished grilling the hamburgers. They're outside on the patio."

"All right, that's what I call perfect timing." They shared a laugh while stepping through Matt's house. But as they headed through the living room Brandon saw a picture that caught him off guard.

It was a photograph of Lisa and him along with Matt and a girl at the beach, having fun under the sun.

Matt noticed his reaction. "You remember that? We all got sunburned. If memory serves me well, you turned as red as a lobster."

"Of course I remember it. Those were fun times. To think about it, what happened to that girl?"

Matt stared straight into Brandon's eyes. "She was swept up with the others." Brandon dropped his head. "Oh."

"Hey, it's cool. She's in paradise. And you're about to be there too once you taste one of my famous hamburgers."

Brandon perked right up. "That sounds fabulous! Where did you say, the patio?"

"That's right, come on." They stepped outside and the place was set up nicely with a table, a few plants and tiki torches burning by a small pool. A plate of hamburgers sat on the table beside a bag of chips and a Bible.

It was a beautiful evening. A full moon lit up the sky along with masses of twinkling stars sparkling brightly.

Matt pointed at a chair. "Have a seat, make yourself comfortable." They both sat and grabbed a hamburger.

Brandon didn't waste a second to put any mayonnaise, mustard, lettuce, or anything on it; nor did he put any potato chips on his plate. He lunged his teeth into the juicy meat.

It was like heaven just shined on him. "Mmmm, this is delicious!" he purred like a little kitty cat.

"I'm glad you like it. I am a pretty good cook if I say so myself. It's just a shame I can't find a woman to cook for," Matt joked.

Brandon responded more seriously, "Trust me, you really don't want one. They're there one moment and disappear the next."

Matt laughed and then realized that Brandon was referring to Lisa. "Hey man, I'm sorry. I didn't mean to laugh or anything about Lisa disappearing."

"Oh, I know that. Sometimes I make a joke. Gets it off my mind." Brandon became quiet. He wanted to ask Matt a question but didn't want to be out of line, so he inquired subtly, "Can I ask you something?"

"Sure, what?"

Brandon phrased the question slowly. "There's something I don't understand. I've known you for years and you've always been a good person and never hurt anyone. You even went to church most of the time. Why didn't you go up with the others?"

Matt glanced at the ground. A solemn expression developed on his face. "The answer is simple, I made a terrible mistake. I didn't take the Good Book seriously."

"I can relate. To be honest, I never even thought about it. But what about now? What do you think is going on?"

Matt picked up his Bible from the table. He held it firmly. "I know exactly what's happening and it doesn't take a rocket scientist to see it evolving. We're in the last days! When I read this book it shows me things that I've never seen before. It's even letting me know what to expect in the future."

Brandon saw the intensity in his friend and knew he believed in what the Bible said.

Since so many people were convinced that something Biblical was in motion, this topic has stimulated his utmost fascination. "Aw, man. I'm so curious. Please tell me what it says."

Matt answered bluntly, "To state it simply, pure hell is going to strike this world."

"I had a feeling you were going to say that." Brandon sighed and then asked the all-important question. "I have to know if there's a chance for me to be with Lisa again?"

"Yes there is. You have a chance. But as the Good Book says, you must believe in Christ with all your heart."

"I've given it a lot of thought and I think it's something I need. I feel a want in my life and it certainly made Lisa happy when she accepted Jesus. Plus heaven sounds like an awesome place to be." Brandon inquired with a bewildered tone, "How do I do it?"

Matt smiled. "It's easy, just say what's in your heart. Ask God to forgive you of your sins and wrong doings and help guide you into paradise."

The simplicity surprised Brandon. "That's all I need to do?"

"Well, first you have to ask in faith. Then you should read the Bible. And man, I'll tell you, it's cool to read. I also think it's very important to remember that Jesus is not religion. Religion is manmade and real faith in Christ is true and pure. There's a day and night difference between the two."

"I totally understand what you're saying and I agree, and I would love to learn what's in the Bible. All I know is I'm so tired of being sad and lonely. I want happiness again. I need a change and I feel that God is it."

"Then follow your heart and do it before it's too late."

Brandon bowed his head. "Dear Lord, I'm sorry it has taken me so long to realize that I need you. But now I believe you are the hope and answer to life. So please forgive me of my sins and guide me into heaven. And please, let me be with Lisa again. Amen."

"This is a glorious day!" Matt exclaimed blissfully. "Now you're hooked up to the main connection."

Brandon smiled. His eyes were gleaming, seemingly relieved of much stress. He had to admit, "This is cool. My heart actually feels better."

At that exact moment an earthquake struck with such power it knocked Brandon and Matt out of their chairs, throwing them to the ground.

An eight-point quake shook the earth immensely. Things were falling from Matt's walls and smashing on the floor. Shattering glass sounded throughout the house as the foundation rumbled. Brandon shrieked, "What was that?"

"That was a big one, it shook the whole house. You okay?"

"Yeah, but that was something. I've never seen anything like that." Brandon laid flat on his back trying to catch his breath. As he stared upwards he noticed several stars falling in front of the full moon. "Hey, check out the falling stars."

But things changed quickly. Thousands of stars began to descend. White streaks were flashing everywhere throughout the atmosphere, lighting up the sky. Then a monstrous blood red cloud rolled in that stole the moon's light turning it into a glowing red ball.

As far as Brandon could see, the land was shrouded in darkness.

Matt shuddered at the sight. "It's happening. It's the sixth seal!"

Chapter 24

Deep in the heart of Nanchang, the capital of Kiangsi, Southeast China, peace was nonexistent. But that wasn't stopping Wong Si from doing what he wanted, and that was selling his illegal tiger potions.

Standing behind the counter in his old store, it struck him he hasn't had a customer in over thirty-minutes. He yelled angrily, "Where are all my customers?"

Wong Si held a long slim bamboo stick in his right hand and slapped it across the counter top, which accidentally knocked over a can of tiger claw. He reached out to grab it, but wasn't quick enough and the can rolled off the counter. "Damn tiger claw! You're more trouble than you're worth."

Tumbling downwards, the can smashed on the floor which popped off the lid and powder sprinkled everywhere.

Wong Si became furious at the loss of money. He hated to lose profits. "Oh, no! That's three hundred dollars a can."

In a hurried pace, he grabbed his broom and swept the ingredients back into the can.

Wong Si noticed that floor dirt was being mixed in with the powder, except he didn't care. It was just a rip-off product anyway.

After reinserting the lid on firmly, he kissed the cold can passionately. "Who cares if a few tigers died for you or even if you're real, you make me a lot of money." Wong Si placed the can back on the counter as a customer entered the store. "Hello, hello. Can I get you something?"

She instructed him in a revolting tone, "Yes, you can. First, I'll take a can of tiger claw and then you can remove those dirty people from the front steps of your store."

A burning sensation surged inside Wong Si. Now he knew why his business had been slow. Deadbeats were blocking his doorway, meaning they were blocking his chance to make money.

Out of everything he despised, lazy nasty homeless trash topped the list. His attitude was if you weren't strong enough to take care of yourself, then you were weak enough to die.

"Sir, did you hear me? I said I want a can of tiger claw," the woman bellowed.

"I heard you the first time. That'll be three hundred dollars."

"Three hundred dollars," she shrieked.

"If you want, three hundred dollars. If not, go. Go now!"

"Give me a can but I buy here no more." The woman threw the money on the counter and grabbed the can. "You're a rude old man," she hollered as she barged out of the store.

"Who cares," Wong Si mumbled. There were more important things to deal with than some old lady's feelings, and that was the deadbeats outside his store. Gripping his stick tightly, he headed toward the front and heard rustling noises once reached the doorway.

#   #   #

Crawling in the street on her hands and knees, Ae Sun Yi was about to pass out at any moment. Hunger had drained her strength. Even clean drinking water had become scarce in this communist community.

Without any food or water, it was becoming impossible for Ae Sun Yi to find ample energy to go on.

A severe hunger pain seized her body, folding her into a fetal position. She grabbed her stomach in the attempts to bring some comfort, but it was useless. Only food could cure her ailment. She glanced downward and her face was only inches above a pothole of stale water.

As Ae Sun Yi stared longingly into the murky water, she hoped for a glimpse of the life she had dreamed of, but it only showed her weathered reflection glaring back.

Ae Sun Yi gasped at her appearance. She used to be such a beautiful woman with a face that everyone adored. But unfortunately, that wasn't the case anymore.

Her looks had abandoned her, leaving her old, desolate.

Sorrow attacked her spirit. Tears started to trickle down her dirt-streaked face.

A man in the group saw her grief and placed his hand on her shoulder. "It's okay, Ae Sun Yi. We will find food soon."

Another lady said, "I have apple in my pocket with maybe one bite left. Some man throw it on street and I picked up. Do you want?"

Ae Sun Yi stared powerlessly at the lady. She hated to accept the apple, but what else could she do? She was about to starve. "Thank you, thank you, I will take apple."

The homeless woman handed her a three-quarter eaten, totally brown and bruised apple. She smiled at Ae Sun Yi with a mouthful of rotten teeth.

The woman's teeth didn't bother Ae Sun Yi, who would love to return the favor someday. "Thank you, thank you." The instant she grabbed the apple she sunk her teeth into the only bite.

Even though Ae Sun Yi has had fresher fruit before, it didn't matter. She sucked the juices of the aged fruit and in her mind this was the best piece of apple she had ever eaten.

Except things were about to change. A bad omen was headed her way.

As Ae Sun Yi nibbled the outer edges for every tiny morsel, a shoe full of dirt got kicked in her face, throwing dirt on the apple and in her eyes. Ae Sun Yi shook her head to clear her vision, and then she heard a loud noise projecting from above.

She looked upwards to a startling sight.

A gigantic creature hovered above her waving a large tree in the air. The bright sun glared behind making him larger than life.

Ae Sun Yi panicked. She was absolutely fearful of the horrid monster. But then she realized it was only an old man holding a puny stick with the sun blaring behind him. For a moment she thought the great Godzilla was about to attack.

The look of happiness in Ae Sun Yi compelled Wong Si to ruin her day. He hated when somebody was happier than he, especially when that someone was homeless trash.

Wong Si waved his stick as he yelled, "Get out of here! We have no food for you. Go, go." Wong Si pointed his stick at Ae Sun Yi. "Do you want more dirt in your face? Then go now!"

Ae Sun Yi wondered why the mean man had to torment them? Couldn't he leave them alone to be in peace? While these thoughts swirled in her head, an elderly man in the homeless group stood his ground. "Leave us alone."

The beggars disgusted Wong Si. He didn't care if they were his kind or not, Chinese folk or whatever. If they were begging in his street then he was going to teach them a lesson. He poked his stick forcibly into the beggar's chest, knocking the elderly gentleman to the ground.

It amused Wong Si watching the old man tumble to the dirt, but he wasn't finished with Ae Sun Yi. He pointed his stick at her and bellowed, "Look at you, you nasty piece of trash. You should be dead!" With a regurgitating sound, he hocked up a mouthful of lung sludge and spit at her.

The saliva flew swiftly through the air heading straight at her face.

Just before the point of impact, the earthquake struck this area vengefully tossing everyone to the ground. This flung Ae Sun Yi to the side, which threw her out of the pathway of the airborne saliva. It barely grazed her face, so she quickly wiped the germs away with her arm so there wouldn't be any trace of that foul person on her body.

But at that instant something else startled her even worse than the earthquake. Enormous black clouds were rolling in with an impenetrable force, tumbling through the sky like a Pac Man devouring all the light.

Ae Sun Yi was utterly spellbound. The colossal black clouds covered the horizon in pitch darkness, stealing every speck of the sun's bright light. Daylight had disappeared, becoming extinct.

Wong Si stood to his feet. His legs were still unsteady as he screamed, "Oh, no! My ass is chop suey."

Wong Si pointed his stick at Ae Sun Yi. "It's all your fault, it's all your fault. This happened when I spit at you. You voodoo witch!" He jumped up and down while pointing his stick at the sky. "Look at what you did. You voodoo witch. Go, get away from here!"

In a fast pace, Wong Si ran to his store and slammed the door shut. The clanking sound of wood being crammed behind it echoed throughout the streets. He was petrified of that woman.

I beheld when he had opened the sixth seal, and lo, there was a great earthquake; and the sun became black as sackcloth of hair, and the moon became as blood; and the stars of heaven fell unto the earth, even as a fig tree casteth her untimely figs in the wind.
Revelation 6:12,13

Chapter 25

After a long day of spending the entire afternoon looking for a job, Brandon stepped into his apartment and immediately plopped down on the couch. It felt great to relax! But reality reared its ugly head. His funds were running thin and this meant he was close to being flat broke.

As stress started to stir in his stomach, he decided to deal with it tomorrow. It was 6:30, time for the evening news. He turned on the TV.

Watching the television, Brandon was amazed at how the world had changed. They were showing video of downtown Jerusalem under attack: bus bombs, terrorist explosions, dead bodies in the street. In a nearby area, a bomb blew up and they actually caught live footage of a body being blown through the air.

A voiceover stated, "With the several month attack against Jerusalem still underway, the past seven days have brought severe violence."

The view changed to a newscaster sitting behind a large desk. His face showed a forced smile. "Hello, I'm Jason Simms with Channel Eight News. In the top story of the day, the President of the United States is visiting Israel to sign a peace treaty in which the United States will protect Israel from any further terrorist attacks. We will be going live to the signing. But first, let's visit our field caster in downtown Jerusalem."

The shot switched to a field caster who was looking at the buildings to make sure they weren't about to topple. This area has seen numerous explosions.

The body of a dead soldier lay in the street twenty feet away.

The field caster spoke to the camera, "Hello, I'm Sam Abbott coming to you live from the bombing zones in Israel. Due to the massive terrorist attacks against Jerusalem, extreme violence has been inflicted upon the people of this country. Here is one of the many casualties."

The cameraman panned to the dead body and the puddle of blood that encircled its head, then focused back on Sam. "Several terrorist groups have claimed responsibility for the explosions, and they all have one thing in common. Their reason for the bombings. They state it's an act against God and his country."

Three gunshots blasted and the bullets zipped past the camera crew smacking the wall behind Sam's head, filling the air with dust and concrete chips.

The camera crew ducked. Sam's eyes grew in size as he screamed into the camera's lens, "Did you see that? That was close. Jason, back to you, now!" He yelled to his crew, "Let's get out of here." Sam ran to the news van with his crew following closely behind.

The picture cut back to the newsroom. Everyone was flabbergasted from the attack. Their fellow employees were caught in the middle of the battle zone. One of the stage managers cried, "My boyfriend is on that crew!"

Jason stared at her. Confusion swarmed in the newsroom, but he had to finish the report. "That was too close for comfort, hopefully no one was hurt. Now to our top story. We are going live to the peace treaty signing."

The picture changed to the inside of a conference room. Two large tables were located at the front.

The President sat at the head position of the right table with Jack Smitty beside him. The President's staff sat beside Smitty.

The other table housed Israeli's top political officials dressed in military uniform.

The Israeli officials were signing the treaty as cameras flashed abundantly. Reporters and politicians were applauding loudly.

The mediator handed the treaty to the President, which made a smile grow on his face. The final accomplishments of his plan were finally in action.

Jeff picked up his pen, the same that another President had used on a different treaty, and signed his name. When he raised the pen from the agreement, the room broke out in applause.

101

The two parties met in the middle of the arena, shook hands, and held the signed treaty proudly between them.

Cameras flashed wildly. The President quieted everyone. "Thank you. With the signing of this agreement you have witnessed the combined efforts of our countries coming together in the name of peace." The audience clapped while Jeff held out his arms, smiling boldly. "This is just the beginning, now we must bring the world together in peace. And the only way to accomplish this is to form a New World Universal Government!"

Jeff Christensen held the treaty high in the air. "May this be the beginning of a New World Universal Government."

Enthusiastic cheers rang from the audience. The Israeli official quieted the crowd. Once they settled, he yelled, "To the first step of a Universal Government and worldwide peace!"

Everyone jumped to their feet in a standing ovation. All hands were clapping in unison.

The President grinned at Jack Smitty and then faced the crowd. He was glowing in victory.

# # #

Brandon stared at the television, absolutely stunned by the news. What was happening to the world?

The pictures of Jerusalem were shocking enough with the terrorist attacks and suicide bombers that never ceased, not to mention the severe violence that has plagued every corner of the earth. But what was this New World Universal Government?

He has heard stories in the past about something like this and the tales always ended dreadfully. Worst of all, it appeared to be taking place right now.

Brandon's thoughts became submerged in a whirlwind of uncertainty. What did the future have in store for him?

Chapter 26

In the throne, intense heat flashed outwards as the Spirit tumbled in his exquisite chair. John the Disciple instinctively covered his face.

The angel beside him inquired, "Why do you cover your face?"

"Because I don't want to get burned!"

The angel chuckled. "The fire cannot hurt you. You're in the throne of God. There is nothing here that will hurt you."

John lowered his head. The angel patted him on the back. "Worry not, you didn't know."

John glanced up, relieved. "Why is there so much activity? Is this for the seventh seal?"

"No, the seventh seal is the beginning of the next judgments. Now shall come the seven trumpets."

John grinned. There would be more! He was becoming worried that the seventh seal might be the end, but now he knew he could stay for longer. Completely enthused, he stared at the throne.

Jesus stood beside the altar with his hand placed on the seventh seal. Power rumbled in his voice, "The time is at hand for the next judgments," and snapped the seal.

Total silence fell over the throne.

John glanced around but the angel motioned for him to stay quiet. John didn't say a word even though so many questions bombarded his thoughts.

Complete calm dominated the area for about thirty minutes. Then a voice thundered, "Let it be done!" Seven angels flew down and landed in front of the altar.

Jesus stared at the angels, pleased at their mighty appearance. He fanned his arm in the air and seven golden trumpets appeared on the ground before each angel. Christ raised his arm and the trumpets floated into the hands of the angels.

Once the golden instruments were grabbed, Jesus commanded, "Deliver the judgments with full wrath!"

The seven flew away holding their golden trumpets. John was left spellbound.

When he had opened the seventh seal, there was silence in heaven about the space of half an hour. And I saw the seven angels which stood before God; and to them were given seven trumpets.
Revelation 8:1,2

# # #

The first trumpet angel cruised at a speed more rapid than a jet fighter, then he slowed to a stop above the world and blew his trumpet powerfully.

A mound of fireballs mixed with blood appeared in his hand, and the angel hurled them downwards.

Sailing to the earth, the balls of fire and blood were about to bring wrath like never before.

The first angel sounded, and there followed hail and fire mingled with blood, and they were cast upon the earth: and the third part of trees was burnt up, and all green grass was burnt up.
Revelation 8:7

# # #

Albert, an overweight middle-aged man was watering the grass in front of his large house. His Hawaiian polyester shirt hugged his skin as his fat cheeks puffed on a cigar, blowing a teepee of smoke into the air.

He sprayed water everywhere, making the ground far too wet. But Albert didn't care how much water he wasted or how much his cigar smoke polluted the air. He was going to do whatever he wanted and right now he wanted to sing a song.

"Macho, macho man. I want to be a macho man." While singing, he shook his fat butt which made him accidentally lose his balance. Albert stepped blindly into a pile of dog crap.

"Jolene, where is that mutt?" he screamed for his wife.

Jolene didn't answer. She was at the shopping mall spending their money, living the life of luxury while the poor were really starting to suffer during this part of the tribulation.

Albert remembered that his wife was out with her snobby girlfriends, and he longed for her to return home with that dog. Ever since she bought that mutt for a thousand dollars there hadn't been any peace in his house. And this pile of crap would be the last he'll ever step in.

Albert glared hatefully at the mess that covered his shoe. He had to clean it so he rubbed it through the freshly cutgrass. But this only made the crap spread more, smearing his shoe in smelly dog shit.

That was it! By now his blood was boiling. Even his chubby cheeks were turning bright red, but he needed to calm down before he overexerted himself. That was doctor's orders. So he glanced over his perfectly manicured yard.

Somehow its beauty mellowed his anger to a fizzle, and he came to the conclusion there might be a little crap on the yard but it still looked nicer than any other in the neighborhood. He would just start sending that mutt to the neighbor's yard to take its dumps. This way he wouldn't have to deal with his wife or her snobby friends.

Satisfied at the outcome, Albert heard a bizarre noise generating from above. He glanced upwards to a startling sight. A twister of blood and fire was surging towards him, and there was no escape.

Albert blinked his eyes to clear his vision. It had to be an illusion, a distorted image of some sort, except he quickly realized it was reality.

A cyclone of hail, blood and fire smacked him and his neighborhood vengefully, igniting everything.

Albert freaked. Blazing hailstones were burning into his skin, searing his flesh. As the fire consumed his body, he waved his arms to clear a pathway to run. But there was no place to flee. Scorching hailstones were pounding the area, catching all the grass and trees on fire.

Albert screamed in pure anguish. His Hawaiian polyester shirt was melting against his flesh, devouring him in pain. He smacked his body up and down to stifle the flames, but it was useless. His hair was igniting into a puff of smoke.

Running around the yard burning alive, Albert was blazing like a torch in the night as when Nero burned Christians on the stake to illuminate the streets of ancient Rome.

His body collapsed. The severe torture buckled his knees beneath him, dropping him to the ground.

In a last attempt for survival, Albert breathed in deeply to get some fresh air, but only sucked in melting flesh dripping off his lips. The searing heat scorched his lungs from the inside out as his body blazed.

Then the fire and hail bounced from yard to yard like a tornado, consuming the whole neighborhood in flames, leaving Albert behind smoldering to death.

#　#　#

In the middle of a Nebraska farm field, a farmer despised the hard work he had to put in day after day. Sitting behind the wheel of a gigantic tractor, he plowed rows of corn while the radio blared his favorite country music. He found the singer's lyrics very soothing, very relatable.

Two months ago he caught his wife cheating with his best friend so he took it upon himself to kill them both and bury them in the field.

The farmer sang out loud, "My wife done cheated on me with my best friend so I cut'em all up." Delighted at having kindred spirits, his joy was approaching a rapid halt.

A massive fire, blood and hail tornado swept down on his farm field torching the countryside. The farmer saw it coming. "What the hell?" he yelled as he jumped off the tractor and ran like the devil was after him.

His legs were shuffling beneath him but the twister was far faster. It hopped feverishly across the field catching everything ablaze. Then the tractor exploded into a massive fireball that threw pieces of burning hot metal through the air.

From hearing the blast, the farmer unconsciously turned to look, and saw his death coming straight at him.

Several hailstones and pieces of scorching hot tractor metal plastered his body, melting into his skin. The farmer screamed agonizingly. The pain of burning alive was crippling him as he dropped to the ground between two rows of corn, blazing like a scarecrow.

Chapter 27

It was a beautiful afternoon as Brandon drove up a curvy road to the top of the local mountains above Los Angeles. He knew of the ultimate location where breathtaking views abounded in every direction.

The fresh mountain air always comforted his soul, and right now he needed some relaxation. He had to clear his head and forget about the job situation. The stress was about to kill him.

Brandon thought about it - life was so much easier when Lisa was beside him. She gave him hope, happiness, direction and security.

Finally reaching his favorite spot, he pulled to the side of the street and parked. Lisa and him discovered this place many years ago and sometimes they would sit on the rocks and talk for hours. Even though the conversations they shared here were usually not of much importance, they've turned into some of Brandon's most cherished memories: the ones that warm his heart the most.

He knew that whatever he might endure, no matter what this ordeal that has plagued the earth might throw at him, no one could strip away his memories of Lisa. No person had that power.

Even though Brandon was parked at the side of the road, he didn't get out. He just sat there thinking about how his life had changed.

Several years ago he would've never guessed his life would be like this: alone. He figured he would've been married to Lisa with kids.

Lisa loved children. She wanted one, if not two. A little girl and a boy and he wanted badly to make her dreams come true, to fulfill her happiest desires.

If they had a boy, Brandon wanted to teach him to play baseball. If they had a girl, Lisa would have taught her how to dance like a graceful ballerina.

Brandon choked up.

He then comprehended an important fact. It was useless to think about how things could've been because they weren't that way now. He shook his head to clear his thoughts, then got out of the car to stretch his legs.

Taking a deep breath of fresh mountain air, he strolled to a large rock that overlooked the massive city and sat. Staring outwards, he realized that Los Angeles was such a well-populated city with millions upon millions of people. So why did he feel so lonely at times?

He knew the answer. He also knew there was a plan for him.

For the first time today, Brandon smiled. There was something great that awaited him - he only had to find it. And he knew he would find it as long as he searched diligently enough. Especially now that God was on his side, all things were possible.

Brandon picked up a small stone and tossed it over the mountainside. As his sight followed it downwards, he noticed something strange happening throughout the city. Patches of fire were springing up everywhere. Puffs of smoke were starting to fill the sky.

Before he could figure what it was, a small patch of grass directly beside him caught on fire. Brandon jumped off the rock, hollering, "What the hell?"

Chapter 28

The second trumpet angel flew swiftly over New York City to the Statue of Liberty. The moment he reached the towering structure, he came to a stop and admired New York's beautiful skyline of buildings. The architecture was exquisite. But he had to do his duty so he raised his golden trumpet, blew it loudly, and sailed back into the sky.

Immediately following, a large fireball appeared in his hand that he flung at the earth.

The blazing meteor raced through the clouds leaving a breathtaking tail until it plunged into the sea, splashing waves hundreds of feet upwards.

Then something happened. The ocean's water started to change.

As when Moses turned a lake into blood in front of Pharaoh, the ocean turned into blood. But this blood was thick and smelt of death.

It devoured the salt waters, dominating everything in its path. The surface quickly filled with fish that were suffocating in the horrid liquid.

The second angel sounded, and as it were a great mountain burning with fire was cast into the sea: and the third part of the sea became blood.
Revelation 8:8

# # #

As two large oil tankers drifted near each other in the middle of the ocean, the crewmembers were having a shouting match. Curtis yelled at the top of his lungs, "Hey, scumbag. I'm going to screw your girlfriend when I get into the harbor." He stared at his friend, Harper. "You think that slimy punk heard me?"

Chewing on a huge wad of gum, Harper glanced at the other ship. "I bet he heard you. I can't believe he did your sister like that, smacking her around and everything."

"Shut up, I don't care to hear it," Curtis snapped back. His fuse was burning short. "That sorry bastard, I'll tell you what I'm going to do. I'm going to his house and screw his whole family, and I don't care if it's a man or a woman. That's right. I'm going to line them up side by side and screw every damn one of them! I'm going to fuck his whole family for beating my sister, that sorry piece of trash!"

The remark confused Harper. "You're joking about that homosexual stuff, aren't you? You ain't turning gay are you?"

"Hell no, I ain't turning that way. I ought to pop you upside your head for talking like that." Curtis became quiet and stared intensely at his friend. A crazy glare developed in his eyes as he spoke in his sexiest voice, "But if I was to turn gay, you'd be the first one I'd screw!"

In a fast move he grabbed Harper from the back and lifted him off the ground, shaking him around.

Harper's feet were dangling in the air but he fought with everything he had, finally breaking free. Curtis pushed him away and laughed loudly. These two have been mock fighting for the past fifteen years, ever since Harper dated Curtis' sister Mona, the one who had been abused.

Curtis patted him on the back. "I don't know why I'm getting so mad at the punk, he had sex with your girlfriend."

Harper stood his ground. "Hey, don't put that on me. We broke up years ago and I don't want to hear it. Really man, I don't care what she does. It's her life."

"Yeah, I know how you feel. I'm just playing with you." Curtis focused on the other ship, which changed his eyes from a look of friendship to a glare of hatred. His enemy was on the vessel and he couldn't wait until they reached the harbor. "That sons-a-bitch. It ain't right to hurt a man's sister!"

"You're right, I think he needs a whopping," Harper agreed.

"I knew you'd be with me. In two weeks we'll be in the same harbor." Curtis flipped a knife from his pocket. The sun glistened on the shiny blade. "And I'm going to slice out his stinking tongue."

Harper grinned. "Yeah, yeah, we'll cut him up. He deserves it anyway. But that's in two weeks so remind me then. It's getting late so I better get back to work. We'll chat later." Harper headed to the engine room.

Curtis stared again at the other ship. "I'll see you in two weeks, then I'll cut you like a fat pig." While he began to enter the ship's hull, he heard several ship hands scream in panic.

This aroused his curiosity, especially when the ship hands were pointing at the sea, shouting, "Blood, blood!"

Curtis wondered if someone was taking a swim and the sharks had gotten them?

Shark attacks have surged recently, especially since pollution and poaching had wiped out a mass majority of the fish.

Curtis was hoping for a shark attack so he picked up his pace. For several months the guys on deck would make a fast bet on how long the person would last against the fish. Five days ago a rookie crewmember was taking a swim and the sharks hit him, winning Curtis a hundred dollars! He called it easy money.

When he reached the ships' railings, something completely different came into view.

A dark blanket of blood covered the ocean that was spreading towards his ship like a wave of death flowing his way. The crew panicked.

Curtis stared at it in amazement. There was no way it could be real blood so the other ship had to be pulling a prank. They must be reflecting a red impression over the ocean's surface.

That was it, that was the final straw! Now Curtis wanted to punish every one on that ship. If he only had a cannon he'd launch a round over there and blow them right out of the water. But as he glanced over the ocean, he had to admit that their trick was an excellent illusion.

The blood seemed horrifyingly real as it seeped beneath his ship. Curtis shrieked, "What is it?"

Now the repulsive happened.

The smell of rotting blood filled his nostrils, erupting his stomach into nausea.

The ship came to an unexpected halt from the thickness of the blood, throwing Curtis forward several feet. After finally regaining his composure, he stood wobbly on his feet and glanced outwards to a mind-blowing sight.

The blood covered a vast portion of the ocean but stopped spreading just before it reached the other vessel, as though an invisible line had been drawn between the ships.

Curtis searched the waters for an escape route. There had to be an avenue to flee, there had to be. Then a plan entered his mind. He could paddle a life raft to the other tanker. That would surly save his life.

But once he faced the ocean to scope the shortest route, a whale vaulted out of the sea covered in plasma, spewing blood from its dorsal hole instead of water. It fell hard on the surface which splashed a wave of plasma over the battered vessel, like a tsunami of blood surging in.

Curtis freaked. The wave of blood drenched him in a gory hell. He staggered backwards, dazed, and watched the whale splashing around on the reddish ocean, fighting for survival.

But Curtis' nightmare wasn't near its end.

The thickness of the blood swayed the ship on its side, collapsing the vessel. Several crew hands were thrown overboard, screaming the entire way until they splashed into the revolting liquid.

Curtis acted quickly and grabbed the side railing to hold on for dear life. He was dangling forty-feet in the air above a sea of blood. Except the fluid that covered his hands was slick, making it impossible for him to grip the railing.

To his dismay, he watched his fingers slip slowly and they finally lost their grip. He then plunged downward, landing feet first into the bloody ocean.

His first instinct was to splash his arms up and down to stay afloat. But the substance was way too thick. So he splashed his

113

arms up and down even harder, except his strength had faded. Curtis felt himself being sucked under.

In a last attempt for survival, he screamed for mercy. But once he opened his mouth a wave of blood gushed in and filled his lungs in death.

His body flinched several times as he coughed up blood, then Curtis sank to the bottom of the sea along with the ship and whale, vanishing forever.

And the third part of the living creatures in the sea died, and the third part of the ships were destroyed.
Revelation 8:9

Chapter 29

It was an awesome sunny day as Brandon strolled down the beach splashing his feet in the surf. This was a good day and he felt terrific. A couple job interviews have come his way and things seemed to be getting better. He had also been spending a lot of time with Matt and it was fantastic to have his old friend to talk to, to share his thoughts with.

But that hasn't changed his current situation. He never knew what to expect, especially with the recent tragedies that have plagued the world. The news articles that showed daily were enough to depress anyone.

Thankfully the stories weren't bringing him down. He felt a new inner strength, one that gave him happiness again, and he credited Jesus for the change. Plus Matt has been showing him Scripture and the predictions in the Bible, which he found absolutely fascinating.

While his mind drifted into nowhere land, he felt a thick substance flow over his toes.

Brandon looked down and freaked!

The water was turning into blood before his very eyes, and he was standing ankle deep in the reddish gore.

He immediately kicked his feet out of the surf, screaming, "What the..." Without hesitation, Brandon took off running to the sand and plowed his feet in the gritty substance, tossing up mounds of dirt. He was feverously trying to remove the dark liquid, but suddenly stopped and stared outward at the ocean. The whole bay had turned into blood.

# # #

A sign was posted at the doorway introducing the event: Universal Fund Raiser for Peace and Government. Upon entering the lavish room, one could get lost in its decor.

A large stage was at the front with two twelve-foot statues that perfectly resembled the President, Jeff Christensen, on each side. The rest of the stage had the facade of a political fund raising event. A huge table and a podium were located in the middle.

An object was hanging on the back wall above the podium with a black curtain covering it.

Jeff Christensen sat at the head position of the table. Jack Smitty sat beside him, along with a few others beside him. And Smitty was wearing the full religious gear with the robes of a Catholic priest and a white collar around his neck.

The President glanced over the sold out room, loving the sight of a full house. He waved glowingly to the crowd and mentioned to Smitty, "Our time has arrived."

Stepping to the podium, Jeff bellowed, "Hello, my friends, and thank you for coming. I have some terrific news to share with you this evening. It is my honor to officially announce the combining of all nations in the name of peace. As of today every country worldwide has signed an agreement to form a New World Universal Government! A society for the people, by the people. Give yourselves a big hand."

The audience cheered passionately as the President soaked up the affection. He raised his arms desiring to be in the spotlight, to be the center of attention.

Jeff finally lowered his arms to quiet the audience. "Thank you, and here is the moment we all have been waiting for. The unveiling of the New World Universal Government symbol. May I have a drum roll."

A band located at the side of the stage played a mechanical beat while the President pointed at the covered object hanging on the wall. Anticipation grew in the room as the curtain rolled up to reveal the Universal Government symbol, <|>. Outlined in red neon lights, it pulsated on and off, flashing hypnotically.

The audience leapt to their feet in a standing ovation, totally enthralled by the revelation.

Satisfied at the response, the President motioned for everyone to sit. "Isn't it beautiful? And there is only one thing you need to join our wonderful society, and that is to receive your own membership stamp. It's even a free membership so there's nothing to stop you. But first, let me introduce a special friend of mine, Father Jack Smitty from the Church of Tomorrow."

The crowd cheered loudly. With a Bible in hand, Smitty stepped beside the President and they smiled at the audience as numerous cameras flashed throughout the room.

Jeff waved once again, then sat in his chair.

Smitty placed his hands on the podium, glanced over the full auditorium and held up a Bible. "There's a verse in this book that reminds me of Jeff Christensen and the work that he does. 'Blessed are the peacemakers: for they shall be called the sons of God.' Exactly two years ago this man prophesied of this day and told me in detail of everything that will happen."

He placed the Bible on the podium, faced the President and continued sincerely, "I have known you for years, Jeff, and I have seen your works and prophecies come true time and time again. I can honestly state that I believe you are the coming messiah that many religions have spoken of for thousands of years. I truly believe you are the son of God! Jeff, if you are part of the New World Universal Government." Smitty turned to the audience and yelled, "Then I want to be part of it, too!"

He hooked them like a fisherman. Everyone applauded joyfully.

Smitty held out his hands, thriving on the fact that many considered him as a powerful religious symbol.

Jack Smitty had a plan in mind, one that the whole world would soon become aware. He spoke to the attentive crowd, "In regards to the membership stamp that the President mentioned, I would like to show you how easy it is. First, it is absolutely painless. I'll even be the first to receive the membership."

Smitty motioned to a nurse that stood backstage. "Nurse Jane, will you help me with this?"

An extremely attractive woman dressed in a sexy nurse's outfit stepped from behind the curtains. She walked towards him holding a small chromed cylinder in her left hand, something that resembled a magic marker, and stepped beside him.

117

Smitty stared at her from head to toe. "With women like you, I don't know why I swore clerical celibacy." The audience roared in laugher and he stared at the crowd. "I'm a man of God, I shouldn't talk about things like that. So let's get to the main subject, my membership. There are two places where you can receive your membership stamp. One is on the back of the right hand, and the other is on the forehead. That is your decision. Personally, I'll take pleasure to receive mine on the back of my hand."

He put his right hand in front of the nurse. "Nurse Jane, will you do the honors."

Smitty smiled at the audience as the neon light of the Universal Government's symbol <|> pulsated hypnotically above him. Nurse Jane touched the chromed cylinder gently against his hand. Smitty did not flinch. His smile grew even larger. The nurse stepped away. "Nurse Jane, I am still waiting. Will you please give me my membership stamp?"

"It has already been administered," she responded innocently.

Jack Smitty looked at the back of his right hand and grinned from ear to ear. "Look at this, I am now an official member. Isn't this wonderful! And it didn't hurt a bit, it even tickled!"

He laughed lavishly while he waved his hand in the air to show everyone the mark. "Now it's your turn to receive an official membership stamp. Let's all come together and unite. Don't delay and do it today! Thanks a lot, you are fantastic."

The audience cheered loudly, quick to give themselves credit for something they have absolutely no knowledge about.

Conversation filled the room with an array of voices echoing from every corner of the establishment. Numerous people were beginning to walk forward to voluntarily receive their membership stamp.

As Smitty watched the crowd come toward him, he smiled and then glanced at the President. Success was abounding in their eyes.

And he causeth all, both small and great, rich and poor, free and bond, to receive a mark on their right hand, or on their forehead.
Revelation 13:16

118

Chapter 30

Still at the beach, Brandon stood in the sand shocked by the blood that covered his feet. How could this be? He realized that he better put some distance between him and the surf, so he took off running as quickly as possible.

After traveling some distance, Brandon finally drained of energy. He slowed to a stop to catch his breath and glanced back at the beach. The sight was unbelievable.

The Pacific Ocean had turned into blood as far as he could see. He then spotted hundreds of fish leaping out of the blood onto the sand trying to save their lives, only to suffocate.

Could this be a bad dream or a nightmare of some sort?

Brandon looked at his feet. Right then he knew it wasn't a dream - blood still covered them. He figured he better get to his car and scrub his toes.

In a fast pace he rushed to his auto, grabbed a towel from the trunk and wiped his feet clean. It turned the white towel into a nasty red.

Stunned, Brandon threw the rag in a trashcan and knew he better inform Matt about this. Reaching into his front pocket for his cellular phone, he made the call.

Matt answered after three rings. Once Brandon heard the lines connect, he hollered into the phone, "Matt, it's me. I'm at the beach. You'll never believe what happened."

"Well, I'm waiting so tell me," Matt responded. Perhaps his buddy might have met a fine lady while he was out and about.

"I was walking down the beach, just splashing my feet in the water when the whole ocean turned into blood. It was all over my feet. I mean it's gross!"

"You have to be joking?"

"Do I sound like I'm joking," Brandon barked.

"Aw, no! It's coming down. It's the second trumpet being released. Where are you? Are you still at the beach?"

"Yeah, I'm standing in the parking lot on the Santa Monica pier. The ocean is a blood bath. Man, it's hideous!"

"Brandon, listen to me. Get off that pier now! There's no telling what the blood could do to its structure," Matt told him forcibly.

"Okay, I'll do it. I'll call you back." Brandon hung up, jumped in his auto and drove away. As he headed up the pier for the street, people were running everywhere. He had to swerve his car to avoid hitting a few. But he made it up the pier's entrance ramp and once his vehicle reached the main road, all hell broke out. A thundering noise exploded behind him.

He pulled to the side, got out and witnessed the Santa Monica pier crashing into the ocean. People were falling into the blood bath, screaming to their death.

Brandon's mouth dropped. "Good God, this is horrible! What's next?"

# # #

The third trumpet angel traveled over New York, heading to the Niagara Falls. The instant he reached the rushing waters, he blew his horn loudly and sailed back into the atmosphere.

A great fireball flashed in his hand that caused an inferno of fire to sweep over his body. But it didn't affect him. He cocked his arm back and hurled the scorching ball at the earth.

Soaring through the sky, the blazing meteor left a breathtaking tail streaking in the sky until it plummeted into the depths of the Niagara Falls, splashing water high into the air.

The third angel sounded, and there fell a great star from heaven, burning as it were a lamp, and it fell upon the third part of the rivers, and upon the fountains of waters. And the name of the star is called Wormwood. And many men died of the waters because they were made bitter.

120

Revelation 8:10,11

#   #   #

Morning freshness enveloped a campsite in the middle of the woods. James sat inside a pup tent staring at his beautiful wife. She was still sleeping like a baby, which filled his heart with joy. He knew he had to do everything in his power to protect this lovely creature, especially since things haven't been the best.

After the disappearances happened, half of James' office, including his boss, had vanished so they hired several new people to oversee the business. Regrettably James couldn't agree with his supervisor and was fired within a short period. He lost his job.

At that point, everything went from bad to worse.

With violence spreading and food prices soaring out of control, it became difficult to feed his family. His wife even tried to find employment but nothing was available. Then came the last straw.

One evening when they were walking around the block for exercise, a car full of hoods pulled beside them and robbed them at gunpoint.

It scared James badly to have a pistol pointed at his face, so he told the truth that they didn't have any money because he got fired from his job.

The hoodlums stared at the couple in disgust. "You cheap bastard, fire on this," the driver yelled as he shot Renee in the arm.

Luckily the bullet barely grazed Renee but it still threw her to the ground. James screamed for help while the punks laughed and sped away.

The sadistic act shocked the couple, but it helped them conclude an important decision. The moment Renee was well enough they packed everything of significance and headed to the woods to find a peaceful environment to survive. And this frame of mind wasn't unusual. Numerous people had chosen this way to escape the ever-growing uncertainty of the world, to leave the evil driven society behind.

As these thoughts bombarded James, immediate needs took precedence: to get a drink of fresh spring water. He kissed his wife on the cheek and started to hop out of the tent.

She awoke. "Where are you going?"

"To start a fire. Would you like some coffee?"

"That would be nice. Will you wait for me?"

"You know I will. I'll be right here." James stepped outside to stretch his arms. Oh, it felt great to stretch. Then Renee crawled out of the tent bearing a sleepy smile. Her hair was a mess.

"Good morning," he greeted and tried to kiss her, but she stopped him by placing her hand over her mouth. "No, not yet. Morning breath."

James smiled affectionately and asked, "How would my baby like a glass of spring water to brush her pretty teeth?"

"Please. That would be nice."

"Coming right up." Loving the outdoors, he strolled casually to the stream with two cups in hand, stepped in the clear water and watched sand dance over his bare feet. After the cups filled, he took a huge sip and the Wormwood attacked his system, making him gag tragically, then he dropped the cups in the river.

James wailed out a panicked call as his body lost full control. He collapsed to the riverbank.

Renee saw her husband tumbling to the ground like his legs had snapped beneath him.

Without hesitation, she ran to be by his side but James had already turned a dark blue. Foam was spewing from his mouth. But the foam didn't scare Renee from helping her lover. She dropped to her knees and performed layman's CPR. Pressing on his chest, she blew into his mouth with everything she had.

His consciousness partially restored.

James gagged, but used his last breath to warn his beautiful wife, "The water. Don't drink the water." His head flopped over. He died instantly.

Renee screamed hysterically. She looked downstream for help and saw the two cups that James was holding bobbing in and out of the river.

One cup filled with water and sank to the bottom, leaving the other abandoned, alone and desolate.

Chapter 31

Cruising down the road, Brandon was heading home from his new part time job. He was glad the day was over. It had been a long one where eight hours seemed like sixteen, but he wasn't complaining.

He was ecstatic to have employment. Two weeks ago he found a position. Well, perhaps not a position in the sense of it being a decent job. Except he had to find something and he had to find something quickly. His funds were completely drained and his back was slammed against the wall.

Just before he found this gig he was becoming very financially petrified. The classifieds had shrunk to nothing. Finding any employment was tough, especially a job that paid a livable salary.

So here he was, the ex-top producing insurance salesman turned maintenance man.

It was a long way from what he was accustomed, though he had to eat and pay rent.

Brandon chuckled from rehashing a strange incident that took place this afternoon. He was in an apartment working on a clogged bathtub. Pushing a steel snake through the pipe to unplug the line, he felt it get caught on a p-trap. So he crammed the cable in more forcibly.

It freed the line; he was able to push it with ease.

Back in his childhood, his father owned an apartment building and made him help with the repairs. Thankfully it worked out that way. It gave him something to fall back on. The insurance business had virtually collapsed.

Working away on the clogged line, he forgot that most pipes in apartment complexes were connected together. When he thrust the steel cable forward, it slid into another pipe and crept up on a lady that was sitting on the toilet.

As she did her business, the metal snake crawled into her toilet and grabbed her on the butt. The woman thought a real snake had bit her, so she screamed hysterically and jumped to her feet.

Unfortunately she was still urinating and pee splashed all over the wall, covering everything in piss, making an awful smelly mess.

Since the walls were paper thin, Brandon could hear the fearful pleas. He immediately stopped what he was doing to listen more intently.

He had to make sure the tenant wasn't in any trouble: that was his duty as a man.

When he didn't hear the screams any longer, he figured she must have seen a spider or stubbed her toe so he finished the job. Once he cranked the cable in, his office called his cell phone and it turned into an unusual situation.

Laughing at the experience, Brandon knew that something of this nature could only happen to him.

By now he was driving down the street near his apartment and recalled the cabinets were empty. It was time to visit the grocery store. As he pulled into the parking lot, he found a space and then noticed a change on the front of the building.

It used to be named "Value Save", but was now "Universal Grocery."

"Wow, they must have sold out to Universal Grocery," he mumbled as he strolled toward the front door. An advertisement sign was posted in the window. It was the same sign as before but the prices have been slashed considerably, making it a pleasant sight.

The old sign read, "Top Label Liquor – pint size – regular $22.00, Today's Special $18.00." The $18.00 had a red slash across it. "Universal Special, now just $4.00." The same with cigarettes. "Cigarettes – per pack – regular $10.50, Today's Special $9.00. Universal Special, now just $1.00."

"Check it out, they finally have some decent prices. Maybe now I can afford a steak," he stated in mid-stride to the door.

But a bad omen quickly appeared. An enormous sized Universal Government guard stood in the entranceway checking everyone out from head to toe. On the guard's forehead, right above his eyes, was the membership stamp: <|>.

Brandon attempted to walk past him but the guard held out his muscular arm, stopping him in his tracks.

"What's the problem?" Brandon inquired.

"There's no problem, sir. I just need to see your membership stamp."

"Membership stamp? I don't have one. All I want to do is buy some food."

The guard smiled, trying to show warmth. "I'm sorry but you have to be a member to enter." He pointed at another sign posted in the window behind him.

Universal Government <|> Members Only

"For your convenience we have a table inside where you can receive your membership stamp. It only takes a few seconds and it's completely free of charge."

Brandon reiterated, "Let me make sure I understand this. Are you saying that if I don't receive your stamp, then I cannot go in and buy groceries?"

The guard shook his head in agreement. "That's correct. Either you become a member or you don't eat."

"You must be joking? I'll just go somewhere else."

"No, you won't," the guard advised with a salesman's tone. "Haven't you seen the news or read the papers. As of last week the New World Universal Government has purchased every food store worldwide. If you don't become a member, then you don't eat!"

The guard paused briefly to let the information sink in as he stared piercingly into Brandon's eyes. He had been trained to pitch this service.

"Sir, I'll be more than happy to assist you in becoming a new member today. The best is you also get a twenty-five dollar gift certificate and our special prices as of right now!"

Brandon didn't believe a word of this. It had to be a fairytale. His vision was pulled to the menacing mark on the guy's forehead.

125

Its sinister appearance gave Brandon a bad feeling. "No way, I'm not taking that mark."

The instant the guard heard the refusal, he hissed like a rabid cat, "You son of a bitch, wasting my time like that." He became extremely aggressive and blocked the doorway. "Get out of here! I hope you starve, you little shit."

Brandon stood his ground. "To hell with you! Get out of my way."

The big goon pushed Brandon forcibly with one hand and placed the other on his pistol. "Screw you, you little punk. I'll blow your stinking brains out right here!"

Brandon got knocked back several feet but swiftly regrouped his footing. He stared at the guard and instantly spotted extreme rage glaring back.

Right then he knew it wasn't worth pursuing. There was no need to argue over something like this and get shot in front of a grocery store. As the old saying goes – it's better to walk today and live to fight another day.

Brandon hurried away while gesturing with his hands. "You're not worth the hassle."

As he headed to his automobile, he heard the guard yell more threats. But Brandon didn't pay it any attention. If he could hear the voice, at least he knew where the bad guy was.

Once he reached his car, he sat in the firm leather seats and sighed. Nothing was going right. His luck kept getting worse by the second. He then remembered why he was here in the first place. Food. He decided to visit the junky place where he ate last night and then he'll investigate this.

Cranking his vehicle, he noticed that the guard was already intimidating a helpless lady into receiving the stamp. This reminded him so much of the Coronavirus days and how the government and others tried to force everyone to take an unproven and rushed vaccine shot and wear a non-medical mask everywhere, and thank God those days have ended.

But this seemed to be taking to the next level. By what he has seen so far, this was like the Coronavirus lockdown on massive steroids.

126

Brandon sat there staring at the guard and woman and knew the lady wouldn't have a chance against the goon's overpowering methods, so this meant he needed to help her.

Perhaps he could run over the evil person with the car and splatter his guts over the pavement, except that would only get him into trouble.

So he came up with different plan. One that wasn't as effective, but one that should work.

Brandon rolled down the passenger's window and drove slowly to the store. When he pulled in front, he yelled with everything he had, "Hey, lady. Don't you dare take that stamp or mark. It's the devil's work. It's evil!" He smirked at the guard.

The guard screamed wildly and ran after the car but Brandon punched the gas and drove away, leaving a puff of smoke from his tires.

Laughing cheerfully, Brandon knew he screwed up that guy's day.

No person will be able to buy or sell, except he that has the mark, or the name of the beast, or the number of his name. Here is wisdom. Let him that hath understanding count the number of the beast: for it is the number of a man; and his number is 666.
Revelation 13:17,18

Chapter 32

Across the sparkling coastline of Hawaii, waves were growing massive in size. Surf was crashing against the sandy beach in an explosive fashion. Even though it was a gorgeous day, the weather has been shifting from one extreme to the other, and it was giving the meteorologist a headache. They have related these conditions to global warming and the melting of the arctic ice glaciers, but who knew if they were correct.

This was the same media that dismissed the incident when one-third of the ocean turned into blood as some type of illness that caused fish to cough up blood. They also explained the burning of the green grass as a conspiracy by crop dusters who sprayed gasoline over the neighborhoods and ignited them into flames.

But who cared what caused these gigantic waves? It was a dream come true for these two surfers.

Ozzie walked out of the ocean while tapping his head to unclog his ears. "Did you see that flapping seal run into me? I thought Jaws done chomped my ass."

Waynesky pulled his surfboard out of the water. "You're a mama's boy, letting a little seal scare you."

"Little, hell, you must be crazy. That thing must have weighed over four hundred pounds. It was even fatter than your girlfriend." Ozzie laughed and took off running with his surfboard.

Waynesky shook his fist in the air. "You better quit talking about my Betsy like that!" Waynesky chuckled. He didn't care what anyone said. He loved big women, so what. His attitude was the bigger the better, and it takes two hands to handle a real woman. Just thinking of those sexual beauties brought to mind his favorite line. "Baby, once you go big, you never go back!"

Ozzie stepped beside him. "Dude, the ocean has been roaring. You want to go back out there?"

"Not me, I'm too beat. Let's get something to drink. How about a cold beer?"

"Yeah, man. A cold beer sounds great! The last one at Uncle Joe's is a rotten fart." Ozzie took off running with his surfboard to a convenience store.

The race was on. Waynesky was right behind him carrying his surfboard.

At the edge of the boardwalk an old convenience store had been around for at least thirty years and was named after the owner, Uncle Joe. But for some reason it was now, Universal Liquor.

Ozzie was first to notice the change. It stopped him cold. "Hey, look at this. It ain't Uncle Joe's no longer."

Waynesky expressed concern, "I wonder what happened to Uncle Joe? I hope the old man is all right."

The front door suddenly flew open and an enormous sized guard wearing a Universal Government uniform took the post. His body blocked the doorway, making entry into the store virtually unachievable without his permission.

The surfers stared at him in awe. He was massive in size.

But no person was going to stop Ozzie from getting his beer. "Come on, let's get some brewskies." They tried to enter but the guard held out his muscular arm. "Wait, guys, I need to see your membership stamp."

Ozzie showed confusion. "What do you mean, membership stamp? We ain't got no membership here. We don't need one. We've been coming here since we were kids."

The guard evaluated them by their appearance and speech, and they equaled a couple marks to add on the list. He told them politely, "Come on, guys. Don't you know what I'm talking about? It's the President's new program." He pointed at the Universal Government <|> Members Only sign. "I'm sorry, but you can't enter unless you're an official member. And the bad part is, you have to be a member to buy liquor anywhere now-a-days."

Waynesky couldn't confine himself. "What are you talking about? We want some beer. And where's your membership stamp?"

The guard took a second to think of the best pitch line. "Hey, my membership stamp is here on my right hand. And it's the Universal Government making the new rules. I'll tell you, man, they've bought damn near everything and they now own every liquor store in the world. And if you don't join their club, then they don't want your business. But I might have a deal for you."

The guard looked around as though to make sure no one was overhearing, then continued soothingly, "How about I fix it where you two become a member and I'll get you a discount. If you buy one six pack, I'll get you one for free."

Waynesky was quick to grab the bait. "Hey, cool. Free beer. I'll become a member to get some free beer."

Ozzie wasn't so gullible. "Shut up, bonehead." He told the guard, "No way, man. We ain't going for that deal. That ain't enough beer. If we both become a member, then we want to buy two six packs and get two for free."

The guard responded slyly, "You drive a hard bargain, but today is your lucky day. You have a deal!" The guard stepped inside the store and held the door open, retorting, "Come on in, we'll be happy to take care of you."

Waynesky patted Ozzie on the back. "Man, you played him like a violin!"

Ozzie grinned. "Yeah, I did, didn't I?" The surfers rushed into the store with happy smiles, thinking they got something over on the big goon.

The guard stepped outside to reclaim his position. Glancing up to heaven, he laughed boastfully, "That's two more souls I snatched from your lying ass."

Chapter 33

Warm blankets covered Brandon while he slept soundly in bed. Then something happened. The alarm clock blared beside his head, jolting him awake. His hand slapped the off button. "Be quiet, it's Sunday morning." By instinct he reached over to search for something, perhaps a familiar touch, and his hand landed on a fluffy pillow.

Brandon hugged it close to his body and drifted back to sleep.

To his dismay, he accidentally pushed the snooze button instead of the off. The alarm sounded again in exactly nine minutes.

Brandon yelled in a dazed state, "What's the matter with you? Can't a man get some sleep?" He hit the alarm button again, but this time he checked to verify it was off. Glancing that way, he caught sight of a picture of Lisa that sat on the table near the clock. Her image knocked the sleepiness away.

Coldness shrouded his heart. How he still longed for her.

Sometimes the mornings were the toughest part of the day, to wake up and see that Lisa wasn't there. But somehow he has to get past it. He has to move on. Maybe he should put all her pictures away, or even start dating.

Several people have told him to date again, even Matt has mentioned it, but he knew he couldn't give his heart to another woman. At least not at this point, and it wouldn't be right to play with someone's emotions.

So his challenge was to find a way to be with Lisa, and if there was a will there had to be a way.

Brandon caressed the picture against his chest. "I miss you so much. How did this happen?" His thoughts drifted to one of his office's yearly camping trips. The whole gang was sitting beside a blazing campfire as he told a ghost story, trying to be super scary, but flopped miserably. Everyone booed when he finished.

Matt boasted, "That was a terrible story!"

"Then let me hear you do better," Brandon combated.

Matt accepted the challenge. His eyes were flickering as he told them a story about a group of ferocious bears that mauled several campers just a few miles from their campsite.

Brandon loved every minute. A scary tale about crazed bears was all he needed to concoct a plan.

Once Matt finished the tale it was lights out, time to hit the sack.

As Brandon was getting situated in his sleeping bag beside Lisa, he snickered because he had to use the bathroom again from drinking too much cold beer. He mentioned while reaching for the tent's zipper, "I have to water the grass so keep your ears open. Matt's story about the bears is true and it happened close to here. But I'll be outside so you don't have anything to worry about. Well, that's if a bear doesn't get me first." He left in a hurry from knowing his last remark would leave her deep in thought.

Brandon stepped by a nearby tree to take care of business while humming a low-key song so Lisa could hear him. But he was also scanning the ground to find a tree branch: a tool needed to fulfill his plot.

A perfect stick came into view, one that was thick and crooked like a bear's claw. Brandon finished peeing, stopped whistling and picked up the stick.

In a sly maneuver, he snuck beside the tent with the stick in one hand, a flashlight in the other and waited silently. Lisa called, "What's taking you so long?"

He didn't respond.

She called again, "Brandon, where are you?"

Still no answer, so she gave it one last try. "Brandon, if you don't answer me I'm coming out there right now!"

After not getting a response, she headed to the tent's door.

The moment Brandon heard movement he clawed the stick against the tent, growled fiercely like a bear and shined the flashlight behind him that projected a reflection on the tent. Lisa screamed fearfully from thinking a real bear was attacking.

Of course the disturbance alerted the other campers. They shined their flashlights and spotted Brandon standing by the tent in his white underwear looking silly.

Laughing at the memory, Brandon glanced at Lisa's picture. "How about this? Since it's Sunday morning and you liked church, let's visit the one they built down the road."

He kissed the picture, got out of bed and headed down the hallway. A spark of life was surging in every step.

Chapter 34

Brandon sat comfortably in his automobile while driving through his neighborhood. The lumbar seat supported his lower back and it felt terrific. As he turned on the radio, he drove by a burnt out church that hadn't been demolished yet. A few months ago he remembered an article in the local newspaper that stated the preacher was delivering a sermon when he and most of the congregation were Raptured, or swept up to heaven.

The church's biggest hypocrite got left behind, leaving an eyewitness to recount the event. "I was sitting there thinking that Roseanne has been wearing the same ugly hat for the past three weeks, and then it happened. It was like they all became glorified and floated away. I even saw the preacher man go up. He was hooting and hollering like he won the lotto or something."

The woman's narrative made Brandon smile, and then he recalled the news clips that followed a couple weeks later. The awful live footage of that beautiful building burning to the ground, set ablaze in an unsolved crime.

This made him focus on how much he screwed up by denying God. Because of that decision he was stuck here with all hell breaking out while the best part of his life was in paradise.

Brandon shook his head. He had to overcome these thoughts. Then again, that was why he was going to church, to learn the truth of God.

After a few miles Brandon arrived at the government building of worship. It had been around for about a year and he had driven past it several times, but never felt drawn.

The place didn't have an inviting allure to any degree. That also transcended to the parking lot.

Once he pulled in, he couldn't believe how full it was.

He finally found a space, walked to the building and entered a large entrance area. A cute usherette was greeting people.

Brandon asked, "Hi, this is my first time here. Do I just walk in and find a seat, or what's the procedure?"

"Are you by yourself today?"

"Yes, I am."

She smiled seductively. "If you would like to sit down front, I believe there's one seat left."

"That'd be wonderful. Thanks."

She rubbed her hand down his arm. "Follow me, I'll find you a nice place."

Brandon followed her down the aisle. He instantly noticed how crowded the building was. People were everywhere, even standing around the outer walls.

As they reached the front, people were starting to stare in wonderment at who he could be to receive such a good location – a seat directly in the middle of the second row.

The usherette slid her body close to his. "How do you like this seat?"

Surprised by the location, he responded, "Sure, this is great. Thanks a lot."

She grabbed his right buttock and squeezed gently. "My name is Scarlett, you can thank me later." She walked away, smiling.

Brandon couldn't believe it. What just happened? The girl actually pinched his butt in the middle of a church! Hopefully it wasn't a sin that would strike him down.

Shaking it off, Brandon stepped to his seat and checked out the building. He couldn't put his finger on it but an uncanny feeling devoured the place, then he discovered why.

There wasn't a Cross or anything related to Jesus in the whole structure. Then the stage curtains opened which exposed the platform.

Behind the pulpit, in the middle of the stage where a choir should be, stood a large statue of the President. It sat on a white stone base with the mark, <|>, painted in dark red.

At the other side of the stage were three purple velour chairs. The minister of the church sat in the middle chair, Jack Smitty at his right, another man on his left.

The organist began to play. The minister stepped to the pulpit and welcomed the large congregation, "Good morning, and it's nice to see you. I'm happy we have a full house because if you remember last week's sermon, then you know we have a special guest this morning. And I can't wait to introduce this person. He's a personal friend of mine who traveled all the way from Washington D.C. just for you. It's the President's right hand man, father Jack Smitty!"

Smitty wore his signature Catholic priest outfit with the white collar and stepped to the pulpit, shook the minister's hand, and the minister seated himself.

Smitty smiled joyfully while waving to the crowd. "Hello, my friends. And thank you for inviting me. When you look around you will notice something slightly different, yet something quite beautiful." He pointed at the statue. "A statue made in the image of our new messiah. There is a question that I have been asked several times this morning. 'Why is there a statue of the President and not one of Jesus?' This is a valid question and I'd like to answer it. Don't you remember when Jesus took all of his own children but left you behind? And after that all hell broke out!"

Smitty stopped abruptly to give his words more impact. Numerous sighs of bewilderment filled the air. "Now tell me, my friends, what did Jesus do for you? He left you behind and forgot about you. But God hasn't forgotten you. He sent us his other son. For God has sent us Jeff Christensen!"

Several people applauded. Smitty stretched his arms to the statue, bowed his head and looked back at the congregation. Tears were forming in his eyes. "Last night, I received a vision. Last night God came into my heart and gave me the power to bring life unto the image. He told me this statute has a life saving message for you."

Smitty faced the statue and screamed, "Fulfill your prophecies in me by bringing life unto the image."

The statue began to move, magically turning and twisting its head. Its shoulders rolled noisily as its eyes glowed in a bright red.

Brandon stared in utter disbelief. The rock statue was physically coming to life.

The statue pointed his right arm at the congregation and spoke hauntingly, "Listen to me. Receive the mark now, or die." It twisted its head from side to side while it stared intensely at the body of people.

An overweight man sitting in the first row directly in front of Brandon jumped to his feet, obviously upset by the spectacle. "What is this crap? This has to be a trick."

Somehow, the statue heard the protest and pointed its fingers at the man. "You believe not in my words, then die." A large fireball flew from the statue's hand that smacked the guy in his chest, throwing him backwards several feet.

Unfortunately, his body landed in the middle of Brandon's lap like an oversized duffle bag.

Brandon freaked. What was it this time?

He squirmed with all his might trying to free himself as several women beside him screamed bloody murder. But Brandon was pinned. The fat guy's body covered his completely and the chair's armrest had him cornered on both sides, leaving no room for movement.

He felt trapped, closed in, ensnared. All he could see was the obese body dying on top of him.

Then something atrocious happened.

The smell of burning flesh swallowed him, filling Brandon's nostrils in the aftermath of burnt skin. He fought hard for an escape route by forcing his head through an opening.

He was finally able to see over the person, and the sight was horrendous. Sprinkles of fire were burning in the man's upper torso like fireworks or sparklers flashing in his chest. His flesh was bubbling from the heat of the fireball.

Brandon panicked, using everything he had to push the body away. But he couldn't, it was too heavy!

Luckily, a few guys sitting nearby joined in and together they threw the body to the floor. Landing with a loud thump, it rolled on its back.

Smoke streamed from the person's chest while he flopped on the carpeted floor a few times and died. His eyes showed the darkness of death.

Jack Smitty took full control of the situation. Anger was fuming in him. "I told you not to doubt the new messiah." He commanded the church guides, "Ushers, remove this nonbeliever. Remove him now!"

Four identically dressed men ran to the body. One threw a blanket over it and they dragged it out the side door.

Smitty sneered, "I told you the new messiah speaks the truth. God also told me if you don't believe in my words." He raised his right arm as a large fireball flashed in his hand, one that produced severe heat, and he screamed, "Then you shall burn!" Smitty threw the blazing ball against the wall where it burst into a thousand pieces.

Embers sprinkled over the audience, filling the building in sparks of fire.

Brandon rubbed his eyes to make sure this wasn't a bad dream. Except he knew it wasn't. The gruesome stench of burnt flesh still hung in the air. No dream could imitate that smell, not even a dream from hell.

He glanced at the pulpit. Smitty looked fully enraged, which made Brandon state heatedly, "This person isn't a man of God. He's evil and must be stopped."

And he doeth great wonders, so that he maketh fire come down from heaven in the sight of men. And he had the power to give life unto the image of the beast, that the image should both speak and cause anyone that worships not the image of the beast to be killed.
Revelation 13:13,15

Chapter 35

Standing in his kitchen, Brandon was still shocked by what happened at the government building of worship this morning. After watching that man die and smelling the burning flesh, he was surprised he had an appetite.

But with his stomach anything was possible!

Probing the almost empty cabinets, there wasn't much to choose from: a couple cans of soup and a can of spinach. As he pushed them to the side, someone knocked on the front door.

Who could it be?

Brandon wasn't expecting anyone, so he walked over, looked through the peephole and opened the door. A teenager was selling newspapers.

The paperboy wore an old T-shirt and ripped jeans. A newspaper bag was draped over his shoulder.

Brandon straight away noticed something unusual about the kid. It stood out worse than a broken nose.

The teenager had the Universal mark stamped in the middle of his forehead, right above his eyes. A matching mark was printed on the newspaper bag.

The boy smiled with a crooked grin. "Hello, sir. Would you like to buy a subscription to the Universal Times?"

"The Universal Times. What happened to the L.A. Times?" Brandon questioned.

"They're gone, the Universal Times took them over. So would you like to start with a three month or a six month subscription?"

"Hey, not so quick. I don't want any subscription."

Once the kid heard the refusal, his attitude changed into a little terror. He sized Brandon up from head to toe and remarked forcibly, "You want to play hard ball, huh? Since they told me to get everyone's business, I'll tell you what I'm going to do. I'll give you a free copy today and be back next week for the order."

Brandon couldn't believe the boy's intimidation methods. Who taught him these tricks? "Give me the free paper, kid. I have a feeling it's the only way to get rid of you."

"Yes, sir. It is." The boy gave Brandon a paper and stared him in the eye. "I'll see you next week!" The paperboy headed to another apartment or perhaps his next victim.

While closing the door Brandon just decided the next time someone knocked unexpectedly, they could keep on knocking. He wasn't going to open the door.

He stepped to the couch, sat and opened the paper as he felt the longing to see a pleasant article about someone helping to save another, but what he saw was quite different.

The headlines spoke for themselves. "The amazing Presidential statue speaks – Take mark or die. People considered as rebels for refusal to receive the Universal stamp."

Panic consumed him. This was becoming very serious.

At first it was the struggle and heartache over Lisa vanishing, but this was a different type of fight. This was war. With headlines that stated, "Take mark or die," meant something deadly could be on the horizon.

What did the job market look like? His was only part-time and would be ending shortly. Shuffling through the sections, he acquired a slight feeling of comfort when he noticed how thick the classifieds were.

He then read the ads more thoroughly, which changed his sense of contentment into one of apprehension.

"Aw, man! This isn't good. Almost every ad states you must have the mark to apply. So if you can't work or purchase any food without the mark, then you're basically trapped. There has to be a way out."

Chapter 36

Traveling swiftly through the sky, the fourth and fifth trumpet angels smiled proudly. They knew it was their turn to rock, so the fourth angel blew his trumpet powerfully. He then flew to the gateways of heaven.

The fourth angel sounded, and the sun and the moon and the stars lost one third of their light. In which one third of the day was without light, and also one third of the night.
Revelation 8:12

The fifth angel headed toward Washington D.C. About ten miles from the White House, he spotted a billboard that advertised an upcoming White Power KKK Rally.

The warrior of God stared disgustingly at the sign, but it also filled his heart with joy. This would be the perfect location to release his judgment, one that would sting the world.

The angel blew his golden trumpet loudly as he sailed in the sky, parting the clouds around him. At that moment, a large fireball flashed in his hand and he hurled it at the earth.

Fire tails were streaking in the sky until the blazing ball smashed into a parking lot. Landing between two cars, it ripped a hole in the earth at least twenty feet in diameter.

The fifth angel sounded, and I saw a star fall from heaven unto the earth. And to it was given the key of the bottomless pit. And it opened the bottomless pit; and there arose a smoke out of the pit,

141

as the smoke of a great furnace; and the sun and the air were
darkened by the smoke of the pit.
Revelation 9:1,2

Dark smoke flowed from the hole, consuming the sky. Then the concrete blew out another twenty feet, throwing several cars through the air like they were toys.

An ungodly pit was reveled, and then the true horror began to appear.

Demonic locusts flew out of the abyss, filling the sky. There were millions upon millions, numbering so many they turned the bright sky black.

Shaped viciously, the locusts had an appearance that only satan could design. Their teeth were razor sharp with dark stringy antennas flowing over their body.

But their main power lay in their tail. The tip had a large stinger that resembled a scorpion's, and that stinger delivered excruciating pain.

The locusts were commanded not to kill but to torment people for a five-month period. Soaring out of the bottomless pit, they began their search for the perfect location to commence their devastation.

There came out of the smoke locusts upon the earth: and unto
them was given power, as the scorpions of the earth have power.
Revelation 9:3

\#   \#   \#

The city streets were crowded in Washington D.C. for the Ku Klux Klan Rally. Racists were present from every part of the country. When the disappearances happened, racist and radical groups of all kinds spread throughout the nation.

At first, street gangs ruled America as the Muslim religion grew rapidly in several areas worldwide. Then the organized groups took over in United States and now most were here supporting this convention.

The white supremacists rose the swiftest from raising the highest amount of capital. Even large businesses were openly donating to the radical groups, giving them the same finances as their political counterparts.

An enormous platform was setup at the front of the rally with dozens of men and women sitting in chairs that lined the wall, all happy to be involved in the event.

The Universal sign hung on the back wall. Flashing hypnotically, it pulsated its bright light towards the audience.

Directly underneath the sign was a large white banner with the words printed in dark red.

WHITE POWER <|> REVIVAL RALLY

Throughout the crowd, most participants wore regular clothes but some were dressed from Ku Klux Klan robes to shorts with no shirt, and everyone was yelling happily. Several people waved homemade signs: White Power, KKK Rules.

The street was blocked off. Behind the barricade stood a group of antiracist protesters and they were about as vocal as the larger group. A man near the front shouted, "God hates racists! You will be judged for this." He held up a sign along with other protesters doing the same. Their signs read: Turn to God, End Racism.

A camera crew near the protesters was filming the event. Then all attention focused to the platform as a speaker walked on stage wearing a Ku Klux Klan uniform. He approached the podium, stretched his arms to the huge crowd and bellowed, "Hello, my brothers and sisters. All I have to say is, 'White Power Rules!'"

The racist crowd broke out into a screaming cheer as the Universal sign flashed above the speaker's head.

The Klansman yelled, "Everybody, let me have your full attention. It is my honor to formally introduce the Grand Marshal of our White Power Rally. And it's the President of the United States of America, Mr. Jeff Christensen!"

The racists roared, "Jeff Christensen, Jeff Christensen. He's our man!" The President entered the stage, smiled at the warm welcome and waved gladly. Once he reached the podium, he gave the Klansman a firm handshake and posed while cameras flashed wildly.

The Klansman gestured to the crowd and headed off stage to find his partner.

While the President adjusted the microphone, the camera crew was shooting footage of the magnitude of the audience. Then the lead reporter, Maria Sanchez, pointed at the stage and asked Robert, her cameraman, "Is that Jack Smitty walking on stage?"

Robert panned to a close up and easily spotted Smitty strutting across the platform wearing his usual priest outfit. Smitty sat in the front lead seat beside the other sponsors of the event. Robert noticed that every person on the stage wore a campaign pin on their clothes. The pin had the Universal <|> mark printed in dark red over a white background.

Robert responded, "You're right, Maria. That is Jack Smitty. To be truthful, I don't know about that guy."

Maria agreed, "I know what you mean, he seems a little shift..." Her comment was cut short by the President's voice blaring through the sound system. "Hello, my comrades. And welcome! Last week someone asked for my opinion. They asked if believing in white power is a racists lifestyle?"

Jeff looked over the crowd and shouted, "And my answer was, hell no!"

The audience went crazy.

The President held out his arms. "I personally believe that your lifestyle is your choice. In other words, whatever makes you feel good is okay with me. Do you people feel good?"

The racists jumped around, loving every minute. For once they had found someone with political power who agreed with their philosophy. The coldhearted racists waved their signs proudly.

At the other side of the street the protesters were doing an outstanding job of booing.

The camera crew was capturing everything when a protester behind Maria hollered, "Racists will be tormented by the wrath of God's judgments!"

Maria heard the comment and instinctively looked for the person. She wanted to get an interview. Statements like that have been hot in the headlines.

Suddenly, a loud pounding sound drowned everything out. It surrounded the crowd but no one could tell where it was originating. Both the racists and protesters became quiet as they searched for the location of the noise. It kept growing intensely.

Then a hint to the noise was revealed.

Rolling black clouds covered the nearby streets just before all pandemonium broke out.

The massive army of locusts soared out of the darkness heading towards the crowd. Millions upon millions of evil bugs filled the sky as the trumpeting sound of their wings brought fear to all.

# # #

The Klansman who introduced the President stood on the ground near the front of the platform talking to his partner about the photos of him and Jeff in friendly unison. Together they planned to spread the pictures throughout the press and Internet. And with the President on their side, they were guaranteed to enlist thousands of new recruits.

Ecstatic at the outcome, the two Klansmen smiled at each other. Now the noise roared around them.

They looked up in confusion and saw the army of bugs at the same moment.

The locusts were swooping down out of the sky thrusting their stingers into whatever they could. If it was flesh, it was game.

A locust set his focus on a swastika symbol tattooed on a skinhead's neck. Dive-bombing the emblem tail first, the evil bug had to join his hateful friend by hitting the nazi insignia dead center. The racist grabbed his neck like someone had stabbed him in a prison shower. He wailed painfully. Then dozens of bugs smothered his body which threw him to the ground in pure anguish.

Participants in the crowd were screaming hysterically while attempting to flee the torturing insects, but it was useless. There were far too many bugs for any escape.

145

As the locusts swarmed in the air, many targeted their next victim. The President's new friend, the Klansman announcer.

A large group came together to attack the Klansman. They hit him hard, covering his torso in black bugs. At least one hundred stingers penetrated his body, shooting venom, and the massive influx of poison caused his eyeballs to bulge from the pressure.

The Klansman panicked as he smacked at his face to clear the bugs. He was screaming profusely from the pain, but the next sight stunned him quiet.

Two locusts landed on his face and clamped their sticky legs on his cheeks. In unison, they lifted their scorpion tail high and zapped their stinger powerfully into his eyeballs.

Venom flowed into the Klansman's eyes until they exploded inside his head, blowing his retinas out of his skull. Blood squirted in streams from his eyeless sockets as the Klansman flopped to the ground, quivering from the aftermath of the trauma.

Satisfied, the locusts flew away searching for new prey.

#   #   #

By the antiracist side of the rally, the crowd stood in shock. The dreadful events were happening directly in front of them, so close it was impossible to evade the screams of the tormented.

At the front of the group a married couple was huddled together watching in astonishment. The locusts were striking the racists, but they haven't even brushed against the protesters.

It was incredible. Hundreds of bugs had flown up to them but they turned to attack the other group, leaving them unharmed. While the protesters witnessed the torture unfold, the wife cuddled against her husband. "Look, honey. They are not hurting any of us."

He held her tightly. "Of course, they're not. They can't hurt us because we believe in God!"

Chapter 37

With his feet propped up on the coffee table, Brandon was watching television. It felt fabulous to relax after this long week. His TV illuminated the room as he switched through the channels, going from one station to the next. It finally landed on previews of an upcoming movie that looked halfway decent, then the local news cut in with a special bulletin. Their logo flashed across the screen.

The reporter's face showed major concern. "Hello, this is Neil Diamond with Channel Eight News. People, please, this is a serious warning. We are about to show some extremely gruesome but real pictures. You should use parental discretion."

The pictures flashed immediately, leaving no time for parental control.

The film clips were graphic shots of half dead people expanded in size from the poison of the scorpion style stingers. Many people were soaked in blood from the attack.

The view switched back to the newscaster. "The pictures you are witnessing happened in Washington D.C. a few minutes ago. This is a full alert. Repeat. This is a full alert. There have been several reported sightings of these ..." He stopped unexpectedly to phrase it properly. "I don't know, dangerous locusts I guess. But whatever they are, there have been numerous sightings in Arizona and by the tracking radar they are heading toward the Los Angeles, Southern California area."

The report astonished Brandon. He then heard something smashing against his living room window.

At first the tapping started individually, and then it grew into a steady pounding like something was attempting to break in.

Brandon looked at the window. The noise kept growing in fierceness. He wasn't sure if he wanted to investigate, but his curiosity was getting the best of him.

Just as he stood from the couch, the TV Emergency Signal blared loudly, causing a deafening distraction.

Brandon stared at every corner of his apartment, completely baffled. What plan of action should he take? The thundering noise surrounded him.

# # #

The night's darkness draped the city streets of New Jersey as the smell of spray paint lingered in the air. A gang of thugs was marking their territory down a graffiti infested alley by painting their symbols on the walls.

The leader of the pack, Montro, shook his can. "This can is empty. Holo, get me another one."

"Why you always ask me? You got two hands," Holo responded inanely.

"Shut up and get my cans. That's your job!" Montro snapped back. He wasn't going to take any crap from Holo.

Holo put his head down. He didn't want to go against Montro, so he did what he was told. He pulled out two cans. "What color you want? Red or yellow?"

"Give me the red, I've found the perfect job for it."

Holo tossed the can and Montro caught it in midair. Shaking it vigorously, he sized up the current image painted on the wall. It was a rich gold colored Cross with the words printed above: "God is #1".

Montro stared hatefully at the statement. "Hey, look at this. I think this is a lie so why don't I do this." He painted over the words, "God is a piece of crap!"

Montro smiled at his girlfriend trying to impress her. He pulled out a pint bottle of whiskey from his back pocket and gulped a mouthful.

As the liquor flowed down his throat, it gave him the false illusion of super strength. "God thinks he is bad. He ain't nothing." Montro yanked a pistol from his waistband and shot several rounds

148

into the air. Fireballs flashed from the pistol's barrel. "Take this, you sorry shit! I can whoop you."

From the excitement coming down so hastily, the other hoodlums gladly participated. Holo pulled his pistol. "We can kill you," he yelled, shooting bullets everywhere into the sky.

Dreg sat on the hood of his '73 Chevy, grabbed his Mac 11-380 full auto from its holster, cocked the bolt rearward and unloaded the 32-round clip in about two seconds. Smiling at the proficiency of the weapon, Dreg smirked at heaven, "Yeah, you ain't nothing."

Dreg might have spoken too soon.

A rumbling noise erupted from every direction, as though their words were heard from above.

Hordes of locusts rushed in to strike the gang members, thrusting their stingers into flesh.

As they brutalized the gangsters, the bugs seemed to focus their attention on Montro. For some reason they were very allured to him. Within an instant, hundreds of black bugs marched over his torso like small soldiers.

Montro screamed in pain while smacking them off his face. But as rapidly as he knocked the locusts away many more took their place, totally voiding his attempts. So he shot his pistol in every direction trying to kill them, but the weapon quickly ran out of ammo.

Montro threw the useless gun on the ground to apply all his energy into clearing his face of the sinister bugs. "The pain, I can't stand the pain!" he cried helplessly. By now poison was surging in his blood, distorting his vision to triple of everything.

Montro knew he was losing the battle, and this caused craziness to flood his mind. "To hell with you if you think you can beat me."

Grabbing a knife from his pocket, he flipped it open and thrust it into his stomach. Blood flowed from the wound, but the knife didn't kill him. "What the hell?" he screamed as he thrust the blade back into his gut, trying unsuccessfully to kill himself.

The gang member wailed helplessly. But once he opened his mouth several locusts flew down his throat, stinging his intestines.

Montro dropped to his knees in total defeat.

149

In those days shall men seek death, and shall not find it; and shall desire to die, and death shall flee from them.
Revelation 9:6

Chapter 38

In the lush green pastures of paradise, everything was amazingly beautiful. Gorgeous flowers blossomed over rolling pastures as snow peaked mountains draped the landscape.

A party of four adults were sitting in an open field, enjoying the afternoon.

Lisa picked a colorful flower. "Isn't this flower pretty?"

"That is nice," her new best friend, Jenny, responded.

Their other friend, Marissa, expressed, "Its colors are so radiant." She picked one and showed it to her partner. "Look at this flower, Sammy."

"Yeah, that is cool. But I'm wondering what's happening on the earth. There's a looking glass over there. I'm going to take a peek."

"What's the matter with you? Why do you want to see those horrible tragedies that are happening down there?" Marissa questioned.

"I don't know," Sammy replied boyishly. "I guess it reminds me of the six o'clock news and I always enjoyed the evening news. I'm going to check it out." He walked to the looking glass.

Marissa glanced at the ladies. "Men! When will they ever grow up? Even in heaven they still act silly." The women giggled. "Well, since he's over there, why don't we take a look?"

"It doesn't matter to me. How about you?" Jenny asked Lisa.

Lisa stared at her friend. Ever since the looking glass was mentioned, Brandon dominated her thoughts. How her heart still longed so passionately for him.

Jenny asked again, "What do you think, Lisa? I've never seen the looking glass. Do you want to go?"

Lisa snapped out of her trance. "Sure, I've never seen it either." The ladies stood and stepped toward a round object located about twenty feet away.

As they approached, Lisa stared curiously at its appearance. It was shaped in a circle with a clear bubble dome that stood eighteen inches in height. It resembled a miniature football dome in many aspects.

Sammy was already engaged in what he was watching. Apprehension suddenly crossed his face, making him flinch.

Lisa's anxiety grew. Could she see Brandon in the object? She hurried over and once she reached the looking glass, she gazed longingly.

It was amazing. Lisa was able to see from heaven to the earth as though looking through a clear tunnel. While the adults gathered around the object, the next sight they witnessed was the street gang shooting their pistols into the air. Then the swarm of locusts attacked the gang and stung them brutally.

Lisa staggered backwards. All she could think about was Brandon and how she prayed he was safe and happy.

Jenny noticed a worried look on Lisa's face and put her arm around her friend's shoulder. "Are you all right?"

"Oh, my God. I hope Brandon is okay."

"I'm sure he is. And by what you tell me of him, I'm positive he's getting by somehow."

Lisa smiled. That was exactly what she needed to hear. "Thank you, Jenny." She took a last glance in the looking glass. "I love you so much, Brandon. Please stay strong."

Chapter 39

Brandon stood petrified in the center of his apartment, absolutely clueless to what was transpiring around him. A pounding sound hammered against the living room window and the front door seemed about to explode open.

To distract him even further, the TV still blared the squealing Emergency alarm.

He glanced at the television. The picture was dreadful. It showed live footage of hordes of locusts swarming down the Las Vegas Strip, attacking people as they ran out of the casinos.

The shot zoomed to a close-up on an elderly woman running down the street. She was holding on tightly to a bucket of slot machine change until a swarm of bugs smacked her, which threw her to the ground and scattered her quarters everywhere.

Brandon started to panic. His windows were about to burst open and his front door was shaking. He had to make a choice and there were only two feasible options.

One was to run and hide in the closet, but that would probably be useless. If they could penetrate the windows and doorway then they could surely get him at any location in the apartment. Now came the other part of the scenario, the part he hated the most. Face his fear and see what was out there.

After taking a deep breath, he headed to the window. He knew he better check it out before he chickened out. Placing his hands on each side of the curtains, he opened them slowly.

Then, from nowhere, hundreds of locusts swarmed in front of the window. Brandon jumped back expecting to die a brutal death at any moment. Their appearance was hideous. The locusts were hissing at him with a face that only satan could design.

But they weren't attacking. Why not?

It was wacky, but once the bugs saw him they actually stopped in midair. They weren't trying to burst in to eat him, or kill him, or whatever they do.

Brandon cowered in fear, and then he began to snap his fingers. His mind was clicking like a computer hard drive while he recalled something that Matt had once showed him.

There was a verse in the Good Book that would explain everything.

In a fast dash he ran to the coffee table, picked up his Bible and fanned the pages to the back of the book. "Here it is in Revelation!" he yelled ecstatically. "The locusts were commanded not to hurt the grass of the earth, neither any green thing or tree; but only those who belong not to God."

A wave of happiness engulfed his spirit. He cheered joyfully because they couldn't hurt him.

Because of his faith in Christ Jesus, the bugs were powerless against him!

Brandon hurried to the window with his book in hand, yanked the drawstring and from the action of the shades opening so swiftly, thousands of demonic locusts swarmed in front of the window. Their eyes were glowing in a hideous red.

He glared at them but felt power emerging from within. He knew exactly what had to be done.

Brandon put his Bible beside his face and yelled, "Go in the name of Jesus!"

At that very instant, the bugs took off leaving his domain. Even the doorway became quiet.

Dazed, Brandon watched the mass of locusts fly away. He wiped a few beads of well-deserved sweat from his forehead and stared at his Bible. "Wow, you do have power!"

Chapter 40

The President and Jack Smitty stormed down the hallway in the White House. Jeff barked at his secretary, "Don't disturb me for anything." She lowered her head while they barged into the Oval Office.

Jeff paced back and forth, enraged by the locusts attack.

Smitty didn't seem too bothered. He sat in his large leather chair and turned on an expensive television. He felt like relaxing after the earlier events, but the President stomped by him, shouting, "Damn those bugs for ruining that racist rally!"

A wild glare controlled Jeff's eyes. He had a pain in his ass, and the pain was real. "One of those stinking bugs stung me!" He unloosened his trousers, reached around his butt and yanked out a fiery red stinger, which made his body jerk.

Jeff held it up as poison dripped from its tip.

"That filthy bug stung me on the ass! I'm going to find his family and slaughter the whole damn batch of them."

Smitty laughed at the President from fuming over a little bug sting.

Jeff saw his mockery and that was the last straw. It upset him tremendously, causing his eyes to glow in a devilish red. "Don't you laugh at me, you piece of filthy crap!"

Smitty became livid over the insult. His eyes changed into a sinister red and he hissed like a poisonous snake, but quickly backed down. He knew that Jeff would butcher him into tiny pieces, to slice him like a piece of meat. Smitty's eyes turned back to normal. An attitude of friendship was hiding his true emotions. "Let's not argue with each other, Jeff. You know this will make our master mad enough to torture us both."

His words hit home. Jeff calmed down, his eyes changed back to normal. "You're right. We must stay focused and finish our mission."

Jack Smitty agreed, "Yes, we must. And that is to deceive and steal as many souls from God as we possibly can."

They laughed aloud, obviously enjoying the task that has been set before them. The TV flashed an urgent news bulletin. The picture changed to a live shot of the White Power rally location.

Smitty turned up the volume. "Hey, Jeff. Look at this." The two men faced the television.

Chaos flourished where the attacks took place. Ambulances and fire trucks were speeding in to help the injured. Traumatized people littered the area. Many were still swatting at their bodies to remove the locusts even though the bugs have already fled this area.

The camera focused on an attractive female reporter. "Hello, this is Maria Sanchez with a live report from Washington D.C. As you can see it's total havoc. A few minutes ago killer locusts attacked thousands of helpless victims. What was originally promoted as a peaceful White Power rally was turned into a scene straight from hell."

She paused to regroup her thoughts. The cameraman panned over the disarray. "What you are about to witness is live coverage as it actually took place. I must warn you, these pictures are extremely graphic and perhaps hard to believe. But it's true, Maria Sanchez was there!"

The news station rolled earlier footage of Maria interviewing a group of protesters. She held her microphone in front of a male protester. "Sir, please tell us. What are your thoughts about the White Power rally?"

His answer was short. "I don't like it, lady. That's why I'm protesting it."

Maria shook her head. "That makes sense." She approached an older lady. "How about you, ma'am. What are your thoughts about the President?"

The elderly woman spoke wisely, "I don't like him. I think he's evil. It's his eyes, they are plain mean looking."

Maria didn't have a swift response so she asked a country boy that stood behind the woman, "What about you, sir. What are your thoughts about the President?"

"The President? He's a racist is what he is. No wait, that man is the devil himself. He's the damn devil," he stated with a thick Southern drawl.

In the background, the Klansman speaker started announcing the President. Maria spoke to the camera, "Well, you heard it yourself. But before you make up your mind let's hear what the President has to say." The view switched to the President while he spoke.

Robert the cameraman panned the audience showing their cheerful response to the question, "Do you people feel good?" Now the noise began. The crowd quieted as the sound grew rambunctiously. Robert moved the shot in every direction trying to find its origin.

Maria asked, "What's that noise?"

"I don't know, I can't tell where it's coming from." Robert focused his camera down Pennsylvania Avenue and saw the sky turning black. As he zoomed in, hordes of locusts swarmed out of the darkness heading toward the audience.

Robert yelled, "What in the world? Look, Maria. Let's go!"

"Oh, my God! Run for it." Robert and Maria ran for their lives to the news van. The camera's view shook while the audio captured screams of people being stung. They reached the van. Robert hopped in the rear, Maria jumped in the front passenger's seat. "Put the camera on me," she instructed breathlessly.

He focused on Maria. From his angle Robert could see the locusts attacking the racists through the windshield and rolled up window beside her head.

Maria hollered into her microphone, "This is Maria Sanchez with a live report!" At that instant, a guy dressed in a Klan's robe without the hood ran forcibly into the passenger window. His nose burst on impact, squirting blood all over the glass. His body was covered with locusts that were stinging him ruthlessly.

Maria screamed hysterically at the bloody spectacle, then the pre-taped footage cuts back to Maria staring live into the camera. She shook her head. "Just look at that, it was like a nightmare that came alive." In the distance she saw an earlier interviewee. "There's the older lady from before. Ma'am, are you all right?"

The woman stepped to Maria. "Yes, I am. Those bugs can't hurt me and that's because I gave my life to Jesus Christ! Just like I told you earlier, that President is evil and I was right!"

# # #

Jeff Christensen screamed at the television, "Turn that off now!" Smitty did what he was told; he could feel tension masking the air.

The President stormed his office, hissing, "If that putrid old witch says I'm evil, then I'll show these cock suckers what evil really is. I want every person that refuses my mark to be locked up with the rats. If they think I'm evil now, then they haven't seen shit!"

Chapter 41

A chilly breeze blew across the front door of the Universal Police station. Inside the briefing room, Sergeant Polisky stepped behind the podium. He knew his men would love tonight's briefing. They have been waiting months for this type of news.

Once he placed the evening's assignments on the wooden stand, he felt a tingling sensation above his eyes. Could it be the new membership stamp causing it?

Ever since he received the mark he has had trouble. It itched constantly and he has acquired several migraine headaches. He visited the station's doctor but was told not to worry. They said it wasn't from the stamp and the irritation would be gone soon.

Except it hasn't. It has gotten worse.

Polisky wondered if his men were experiencing the same problem. As of last week it became official policy that every police officer worldwide had to receive the mark on their forehead. They called it a quick identification system.

But it wasn't just the stamp that was aggravating him. It was also their newly issued uniforms. They might be decorated nicely with the Universal Police patches and badge, but the material was way too stiff.

Sergeant Polisky motioned for everyone's attention. "Listen up, guys. I have some special news for tonight's briefing."

An overweight officer, Joe, interrupted, "Hey, Sarge. Before we get started, I have a question to ask."

"Yeah, what is it, Joe?"

"It's these new uniforms. Mine needs to be altered. It's a little too tight around the crotch. Who do I go see?"

Polisky knew it would be something stupid if it came from fat cop Joe, so he squelched the remark. "The only truth in that statement is little, especially when it refers to your crotch. Go see your hand,

159

Joe." Everyone laughed as Polisky continued, "Okay, calm down. I have some important news. The day you've been waiting for is finally here. It's now open season on anyone that refuses to receive the Universal mark."

The policemen responded happily. Polisky lifted his arms. "Listen up, our President issued an order that gives the Universal Officer full authority to arrest any individual that has not received the mark."

Joe loved every minute. This was music to his ears. "All right, it's about time! Can we shoot those believing fools?"

Polisky expected that response. "I knew that question would arise. And Joe, I figured you'd be the one that asked it."

Everyone chuckled while the Sergeant glanced at a piece of paper. "The issue reads as follows: The Universal Officer has full authority to use any amount of force needed to apprehend the unmarked suspect. It is at the Universal Officer's discretion as to the amount of force that will be used."

"So in other words I don't have to wait for deer season to do some killing," Joe crowed.

"No, Joe, it doesn't mean that and that's not what I said. Everybody, listen up. Do not interpret this as a free pass to kill as many of these rebels as you wish. Our job is to apprehend and bring them into custody. The purpose of this assignment is to give these people one last chance to receive the Universal mark."

Joe's fervor was overflowing. "Hey, Sarge. Why waste our time? We should kill them. That way we don't have to feed those sorry rats."

"Sure, Joe. I guess that'd mean more food for you, huh? Dream on." Everyone snickered quietly and Polisky decided to throw them a bone. "I'm going to let you have some fun tonight. First, break yourselves into groups of four, then you decide whom you would like to arrest. No search warrant needed. So if you have an ax to grind, tonight's the night. Be careful and meeting adjourned."

The Sergeant stepped from the podium, feeling satisfied. He knew his officers would fight tooth and nail for him for giving them this type of freedom.

Joe didn't waste a moment to round up his team. "Peter, Yurik, Frank, get over here. It's time to take care of business." A smirk crossed his face as they pulled their chairs together. Joe stared into their eyes. "I know who we should get first. That pecker-head Matt who lives in the hills."

Yurik could never figure why Joe hated that person so much, and Joe has never given a straight answer. So Yurik pinned him down in front of the posse. "What is it with that guy, Joe? You've been talking junk about him for years. What did he ever do to you?"

"That scumbag screwed my wife," Joe growled in hatred.

"You mean your ex-wife. She left you over four years ago," Peter added.

"Shut up, that's besides the point. I don't like the punk and that's why we're going to get the slime ball," Joe snapped back, leaving no room for argument.

Frank squinted his eyes. This cop just heard the words that he loved the most – going to get the slime. During a past drug raid he earned a nickname, Frank the Frankfurter. After charging into a crack house, a drug addict attacked him with a butcher knife. Frank fought the knife from the assailant and sliced him into pieces. Covered in blood, Frank opened their refrigerator, saw a pack of hotdogs and ate one as blood dripped off the uncooked meat.

Callousness filled Frank's voice. "Let's get that criminal and bring him into justice!"

161

Chapter 42

The night sky provided little light as Joe parked the patrol car in front of Matt's house. "That's where the punk lives. This is for the trophy, let's go hunting."

The four cops exited the vehicle and ran up Matt's driveway. Each officer wore a bulletproof vest that had the Universal Police symbol printed on both sides.

Yurik carried a 12-gauge shotgun. His left hand pumped a round into the chamber, preparing for resistance. He hated situations like this. He never knew what to expect. Last month two fellow cops raided a house and the suspects set a surprise for them: ten one-pound bricks of C-4. Just as the crooks escaped via a hole cut in the floor, the cops kicked in the door and were blown to smithereens.

The four men approached the garage.

Fat cop Joe instructed Peter and Frank, "Okay, you two. Go to the rear. The instant you hear me kick in the front door, I want you to bust through the patio door and attack them hard."

Frank looked at his watch. "Give us ninety seconds and go for it." He cocked the bolt on his MP-5k machinegun, nodded at Peter and they scurried to the rear of the building.

Joe told Yurik, "You stand back while I kick that door in." As Joe prepared to rush the house, Yurik said, "Look, Joe. I know you don't like the guy but don't get too crazy."

"Yeah, right," Joe smirked and charged his obese body toward the door like a stampeding elephant, ramming his shoulder dead center into the wooden structure. The extreme blow knocked the door off its hinges, making the pathway clear ahead.

Joe ran inside, yelling, "Universal Police! Raid."

Yurik moved strategically behind Joe, pointing his shotgun in every direction. He always kept his eyes on the furniture and

162

closets. Gang members hiding behind couches have killed three of his friends.

In Yurik's line of work, it was defense, defense, defense.

When Joe and Yurik reached the living room, a lawn chair crashed through Matt's patio door, shattering glass everywhere.

Frank and Peter ran in with their guns drawn, searching high and low, ready for action.

Chapter 43

Inside Matt's house, things couldn't be better. Brandon was relaxing on the couch watching television while Matt sat at the other side doing the same.

A couple of their buddies, Tommy and Andrew, were kicking back at the dining room table studying a Bible. Tommy was intrigued by what he saw. "Hey, guys. You ought to check this out."

"What are you talking about?" Matt questioned.

"It's the six trumpet. Since the fifth has been sounded with the locusts attacking those misguided people, it's almost time for the sixth. And you ought to see this one. It's wicked!"

Brandon had a large bowl of popcorn on his lap. Cramming a handful in his mouth, he enjoyed its buttery favor. He has always loved popcorn, especially at the movies. There was nothing better than a good movie and a bucket of hot butter popcorn. But Tommy had peaked his curiosity. "Well, don't leave us hanging. Tell us about it."

At that very second, all hell broke out.

The front door was kicked in, a large chair smashed through the patio door, and people were running into the house screaming.

Brandon freaked. What was it this time? The ear shattering commotion nearly scared him to death. His instincts kicked in and he jumped from the couch to his feet, which threw popcorn everywhere.

Frank ran in loving every minute. His mind was calculating the situation like a mechanical soldier, analyzing every inch of the room. His attention was pulled to a foreign white substance floating in the air. Frank rushed the suspect. He wasn't going to let a dope smuggler get away from him. "Freeze, criminal!" he yelled as he smacked the metal stock of his MP-5k against Brandon's head.

In Frank's line of work, it was attack, attack, attack.

Brandon's vision blackened. His knees buckled beneath him and he dropped helplessly to the floor.

Matt watched Brandon flop to the ground like a fish out of water. He yelled at the cops to stop and was about to jump in between them, but Yurik pointed a shotgun at his mouth. "I wouldn't do that if I was you."

Matt froze in his tracks. He raised his hands. "Hey, no problem. Keep cool."

Fat cop Joe slapped his nightstick across his hand to produce a menacing sound, then he jammed the stick into Matt's lower back. "Keep cool, huh. No problem. Is that what you're saying, boy?"

Matt grabbed his side in pain. He quickly scanned the officer. The person seemed slightly familiar but he wasn't sure. "Do I know you?"

Joe slammed his nightstick against a glass vase that sat on a coffee table, splintering it into a thousand slivers. "You piece of dirty crap! You have sex with a man's wife and don't even remember what he looks like?"

The remark stunned Matt. Immediately he tried to recall every person he had ever encountered, from childhood to this moment, and couldn't place the guy. What was he talking about? Slept with his wife?

Then it came to him. Matt had seen this person once before, but it was years ago. "Hey, wait, I know who you are. You must be crazy. That was over seven years ago and you just met the girl, you weren't married to her."

"I don't care, you still screwed her! And don't you talk back to me, boy," Joe yelled as he rammed his nightstick into Matt's gut.

The blow knocked Matt breathless, bending him over. He gasped for oxygen trying to catch his breath.

Joe stared at him in disgust, adoring the fact that Matt was suffering in pain. "You always were a little bitch." Fat cop Joe pointed at Brandon. "Get this douche bag out of here and lock him up."

Tommy and Andrew sat spellbound at the dining table. They wanted to help their friends but didn't have much of a choice. Officer Peter stood in front of them with two pistols pointed at their heads. A pistol was in each hand, aimed at each head. The hammers were cocked back with his fingers placed firmly on the triggers.

Tommy and Andrew had their hands raised high in the air.

Tommy inquired of Joe. "Sir, why are you arresting us? What laws have we broken?"

Suddenly there was a new fish for Joe to play with. "Well, Mr. Smart Ass. I'll tell you what laws you've broken. Have you received the Universal mark?"

"No way," Tommy replied spiritedly.

"Then you broke the law, you stupid punk. And you're going to jail for it!"

"I may be going to jail but you're going to burn in the pits of hell, you demon."

The remark hit a sore spot. "Shut your mouth, you filthy rodent!" Joe howled dramatically as he yanked his pistol from its holster and shot Tommy between the eyes, exploding the back of Tommy's head into blotches of bloody tissue. Brains and blood splattered the wall while the echo of gunfire reverberated in the house.

Tommy's body plummeted to the floor as a puddle of blood quickly encircled his lifeless figure.

Joe yelled at the cops, "Get these cockroaches out of here and lock'em up with the rats!"

166

Chapter 44

Cells littered the walls inside the local jailhouse. Guards were dragging prisoners down a long corridor with ropes tied to their handcuffs. Several other officers stood along the walls holding cattle prodders or stun guns. If someone got out of line or if they simply didn't like your face, then you got zapped with massive voltage.

The jailhouse was completely full of newly arrested people, consisting of both men and women of all colors and nationalities. These were the folks who refused to receive the mark of the beast: the prophesied signature of evil.

A guard dragged a prisoner in front of a jail cell, pushed him to the soiled ground and yelled into the overcrowded cell, "You people are fools for not joining the Universal club." He called to the head guard, "Roger, open up number five."

The metal door opened while the guard threw the prisoner into the cold cell.

The captured person rolled to a stop on the concrete floor, barely able to move. He had been beaten badly. Blood covered his hair and he shook frantically. Then the metal door slammed shut creating a deathly chill.

A voice arose from behind the prisoner, "Damn those demons." Brandon, Matt and Andrew were sitting on a steel bench a few feet away with their backs against the wall.

Andrew was angry. "I said it once and I'll say it again, damn those demons." Matt and Andrew stared at the dreadful sight.

Brandon was mainly consumed in massaging his bruised forehead. His expression said it all - what did he get into this time?

"This is a bad nightmare, that's what it is. I'm going to pinch myself to wake up and this will all be over," Brandon tried to persuade himself. He then actually pinched his arm in the hopes of it waking him up. He wanted so badly to be lying in bed beside Lisa, living life like he used to, like he enjoyed.

But life wasn't that easy and the pinch hurt more than it did any good, only multiplying his misery.

One of his best friends was murdered in cold blood and he was sitting unjustifiably in jail. Adding to it, the retched jail had blood, urine and feces covering the walls and floors that made it virtually impossible to breathe.

Brandon's thoughts went to his friend. "I can't believe those dirty cops shot Tommy in the head."

Matt overheard the remark and patted him on the shoulder. "Try not to think about it, my friend. They'll get what's coming to them."

Brandon stared deeply into Matt's eyes. "I hope they get it soon, trying to make us take that devil mark. I can't wait until The Second Coming. Those bastards will burn for eternity!"

Andrew heard the words that he loved more than any other. "That's the truth. The way I look at it, if you die for the Lord, Heaven. If you take the mark of the beast, hell."

Sadly, a huge guard standing near the cell's door heard Andrew. "Hey, you. You can't talk that crap here." He yelled, "Roger, number five. Open it up, now!"

The cell door flew open. The guard ran in, grabbed Andrew off the bench and threw him effortlessly through the air.

Andrew smashed against the steel bars of the opposing cell across the hallway. He dropped hard to the concrete floor, close to unconsciousness.

Brandon, Matt, and everyone in the cell watched in horror. Andrew was tossed like a toy doll. Several Universal cops hurried to the door as the guard who threw Andrew pointed at Brandon and Matt. "Grab those two, he was talking to them."

Within an instant, two oversized cops grabbed Matt and Brandon and threw them out of the cell to the concrete floor. Then four other officers jumped on their backs to handcuff them.

Brandon's face was smashed into the dirty floor. One of the guards dropped his knees into the center of his back, making Brandon gasp painfully, "What's the matter with you?"

The officer grabbed a handful of Brandon's hair and yanked it back to look into his eyes. "What's the matter with me? I don't like your stinking face, that's what's the matter with me." The goon slammed Brandon's head against the floor, cutting his lip on the cement surface.

Blood flowed down Brandon's face as the cops locked a long chain onto the handcuffs.

Andrew was dazed. Brandon and Matt stared at each other and knew this was serious, deadly serious. They had to try something, anything, and both men sprung to their feet.

But the moment they stood they were knocked to their knees by nightsticks.

The officers laughed boastfully as they jerked the chains attached to the handcuffs, dragging them down the hallway.

Brandon, Matt and Andrew were bouncing off the walls.

The oversized guard who attacked Andrew rubbed his nightstick agonizingly across the metal bars. "If I hear anyone else talking that crap, the same will happen to you!" He spit into the cell and stomped away.

A prisoner sitting near the corner of the cell sighed, "This is bad. They dragged away three other people yesterday and we haven't seen them since."

Chapter 45

In the throne of God, John the Disciple was spellbound. The last locusts judgment fascinated him and he truly anticipated what was next. And the answer came quickly. John saw the sixth trumpet angel sailing to the altar.

The Spirit's voice thundered, "Loose the four fallen angels which are bound in the great river Euphrates."

The sixth trumpet angel took off to the earth, heading to the desert outside of Baghdad, Iraq. His objective was at the Euphrates river that flowed through the barren country.

Swooping down, the angel hovered twenty feet above the river's edge and glanced at his surroundings. He held pity for those who would be in the pathway of this judgment: the atrocities that were about to be unleashed.

The angel spit on the dirt, flew back into the sky and blew his trumpet loudly.

At that instant, the ground where he spit exploded open, throwing dirt upwards like fountains of water flowing from the earth. Then things settled down again. After the air cleared of all the dust, a gigantic hole was reveled which depths went down forever.

The land began to tremble. Smoke and ash along with the smell of rotting flesh spewed from the pit, and then the ungodly appeared.

Four satanic beasts rose out of the abyss sitting on the back of their devil horses. Spitting out black tar and ash, the riders and horses were sucking in fresh air to revive their bodies.

Pure death dwelt over them as they emitted an aura of destruction.

The rider's face was horrifyingly hideous, something similar to a satanic skeleton. Burnt red skin covered their scorched bodies as long stringy hair hung down past their shoulders.

But it wasn't the riders that inflicted death; it was the horses.

Designed ferociously, the horse's head was similar to a lion and they breathed fire, smoke and sulfur from their mouths, like a devilish dragon of the old myths.

Their tails were just as wicked.

In appearance it resembled a horse's tail, but it was a snake with the head and teeth of a rattler. And the serpents enjoyed biting to inflict pain.

The demon horses reared their bodies upwards, kicking their hoofs violently in the air.

The four horsemen soared into the sky while their armies followed them from the pit. There were thousands upon thousands, all longing for their chance to bring destruction worldwide.

The masses of demon horsemen exited the pit, flying wildly into the sky.

The sixth angel sounded, and the four fallen angels were loosed who had been prepared to slay the third part of men. And the heads of their horses were as the heads of lions: and out of their mouths issued fire and smoke and brimstone. For their tails were like serpents, and had heads, and with them they do hurt.
Revelation 9:15,17,19

Chapter 46

The city streets were crowded in downtown China. The main priority for most people was survival, just to put some food in their belly. Venders sprinkled the roads selling basically everything from food products to shoes.

A loud commotion broke out at one stand, and it was the mean Wong Si causing the disturbance.

Wong Si stood in front of a vendor's stand that was covered with dead chickens hanging upside down by their feet. He pointed his bamboo stick at the dead chickens and screamed, "Too much, too much. You try to cheat me!"

The vendor stared disgustingly at Wong Si. From the moment this wretched person stepped near the stand, he has been yelling and cursing the entire time. The vendor tried to cut these people slack because it sickened him every time he saw them eat those awful bugs.

Even though the locusts never attacked this section of the Asian continent, they were still plentiful.

Immediately after the locusts inflicted their havoc for a five-month period, they died mysteriously, which left millions scattered over the grounds of several areas worldwide. Major food companies saw the potential and packaged the bugs for sale, producing another avenue to generate revenue.

But once the vendor looked closely at Wong Si, he knew this old man hasn't resorted to eating bugs; he was far too fat around the gut. Wong Si yelled more threats and that was it, the vendor's patience had expired. "Look, old man, get out of here. I don't want your stinking business."

Wong Si couldn't believe that a person didn't want his business. This couldn't be right, only he could tell someone that he didn't want their business. No one could say that to him!

Wong Si slapped his bamboo stick on the counter. "You cannot talk to me that way. I will hurt you with stick."

The vendor laughed. "Get out of my face. I'm not going to sell you shit!"

Wong Si pounded his stick on the counter, but a thundering noise from above stole his attention.

The devil horsemen swooped down from the sky. Flying above the crowds, they were preparing to do their damage.

Once the people saw the beast, panic spread and everyone ran down the streets in complete terror. This made the devil horsemen squeal dementedly at all the helpless victims. They loved every minute, seeing exactly what they longed for: their chance to deliver the same fiery death that they received.

The riders slapped their horse's head to instruct the animals to blow fire from their mouths.

Flames blasted five feet from the horse's mouth like mini flamethrowers, blistering people in tremendous heat. The crowds ran helplessly from being set on fire as many dropped to their knees in crippling pain.

Wong Si saw the army of demon horsemen coming straight at him. This had to be a trick of some sort. But just in case, he backed up several steps and waved his puny stick in the air.

Two demon horses swooped down, landing on each side.

Wong Si was blocked in soundly and quickly realized this wasn't a trick, this was reality. And he was going to teach them a lesson for screwing with him. He slapped his bamboo stick against the demon horsemen, except this only entertained the riders more. They placed their burnt face directly in front of Wong Si's and screamed to put the fear of death in the old man, then they smacked the side of their horse's head.

The snake tail of each horse bit Wong Si on the wrist. One on the right, the other on the left, and stretched him out completely.

Wong Si squealed in pain, but his torment was just beginning. The satanic animals turned their heads inward and blew a burst of fire from their mouths, torching the old man.

173

Wong Si's body began to blaze. Blood started to gush from his mouth, then the extreme heat melted his ears from his head like they were candle wax. Liquefied human flesh splashed on the dry dirt below.

Satisfied at a well-done job, the two horses reared their lion's head upward, roared loudly and blew a burst of flame from their mouths.

Their snake tails let go of Wong Si.

The old man fell to the ground, shaking into convulsions from the aftermath of being burnt to death.

The demons laughed as they flew away searching for new prey.

# # #

Inside the Oval Office, Jeff Christensen sat at his desk shuffling through a stack of papers. He had to plan his next move before another problem altered his strategy.

Jack Smitty didn't seem too bothered as he relaxed in his firm leather chair reading a book. He knew Jeff was in an uptight mood, but this novel captured his attention which left no room for distraction.

While the President scrutinized a document, the lamp on his desk burned out, leaving him in darkness. This pissed him off even more so he slapped the lighting fixture to the floor, breaking it into several pieces. "Stinking lamp, I paid two hundred dollars for it and it didn't last a week. The piece of crap!"

Smitty glanced from his book. "I told you that lamp was no good. I bought the same one last year and it broke on me within a month."

Jeff's eyes squinted as he barked, "Those bastards charged me two hundred dollars. I want you to find out who makes these sorry lamps and have them shut down! Do you hear me?"

"Yeah, I'll do what I can," Smitty agreed just to calm him down. There was no need to argue about a cheap lamp.

The President's door was opened slightly. An assistant knocked gently and poked his head in. "Mr. President, do you have a minute?"

174

Jeff looked from his papers. "What do you want?"

The assistant spoke dramatically, "Sir, you will not believe what happened. It's something straight out of a science fiction movie!"

"Look, boy. I don't have time for your games. What are you talking about?"

The assistant bowed his head. "Yes, sir. I am sorry." He stated more calmly, "We have received disturbing reports from China. Millions of people have been burnt to death."

"Oh, no," Smitty uttered with concern.

Jeff responded much more aggressively, "When did this happen?"

"Approximately ten minutes ago, sir," the assistant answered swiftly.

"You stay on top of this and find out how many were killed. Do you hear me?"

"Yes, sir. It's as good as done. Thank you, sir." The assistant scurried away.

Jeff slammed his fist on the desk. "What the hell's next?"

Smitty's apprehension was obvious. "This isn't good, Jeff. Half of our army is located there."

The President exploded over the comment, "Don't you think I know that, you stupid fool!" Jeff Christensen leaped to his feet. "This is it! I want every one of those sorry rats that refuse my mark to be killed. And I want them killed right now!"

Chapter 47

It was a beautiful afternoon. A gorgeous sun sparkled brightly, delivering its warmth over the world. But to the people being forced to participate in the President's new program, take the mark or die, this was a horrid day.

A shiny chrome guillotine sat on a hi-tech platform at the front of a large area. The <|> symbol was displayed boldly above the killing machine.

The stench of death filled the air, the massacres had already begun. Two guards were un-strapping a headless body from the death machine. They dragged it to the side of the platform and tossed it into the back of a pickup truck.

The truck was now full of butchered bodies, so it drove away as another pulled up to take its place. The stairs that lead to the top of the platform were located at the other side. Beside the stairs was a table where one could receive the mark if they choose.

Several officers holding M-16 machineguns kept a stern eye over all.

A line of twenty people stood in front of the guillotine, folks who have refused the Universal mark and were about to be beheaded for their decision.

The executioner smiled. He couldn't wait to chop up the next three people. Andrew was first, Matt second and Brandon third.

The demons went on the prowl. A guard whose job it was to intimidate others into receiving the mark carried a decapitated human head in his hand. The mark of the beast showed clearly on the guard's forehead along with several drops of splattered blood, souvenirs from the dead. He laughed joyfully. This was a great day. He just deceived a lady into receiving the mark, which meant bonus money in his next paycheck.

By the table where the stamp was given, a lady became frightened and received the mark. She looked at her right hand and cried out loud, then ran in front of the crowd of onlookers.

"Oh, man. I'm next. And I'm not afraid to say, I'm scared to death," Andrew groaned in panic. His breathing was very sporadic.

Matt patted him on the back. "Don't worry, my brother. It'll be quick and then your soul will be swept into paradise. For you shall see God."

"Amen to that. Just think, I'll be able to see my best friend Tommy again and Brandon will see Lisa."

Brandon looked like a wild animal. An untamed glare controlled his eyes. He was afraid and rightly so, but he heard Andrew. "Thanks, my friend. That means a lot to me."

Before another word could be said, the guard that carried a bloody head shoved it in front of Andrew, shaking it wildly. "Do you want to die like this or live in peace with us?"

Andrew stared at the gory object but stood his ground. "Live in peace with you? Have you looked in the mirror? I'd rather give my life than live with you demon infested people."

"Screw you," the guard hissed.

"I feel sorry for your soul. You'll burn in the pits of hell forever."

The remark infuriated the guard. He pushed Andrew toward the guillotine, yelling, "Chop his head off now!" Several officers grabbed Andrew to drag him to the butchering block of the guillotine.

Andrew struggled with all his might to fight them, but it was a losing battle. Two additional officers jumped in and threw him viciously on the guillotine table. They fastened the straps around him so tight that Andrew had trouble breathing.

Gasping for air, Andrew's face was turning a bright shade of red. He was totally defenseless with no way out.

Brandon and Matt were startled by what happened, and by how swiftly it transpired. Their friend was about to meet a tragic death, so they stared intensely at Andrew to hopefully bring him some type of comfort.

Matt was first in line, standing tall. His eyes showed the look of total faith. He thought about it. At least the guillotine would be a swift death. But most importantly, right at this very instant he knew the ultimate feeling to fight for his faith, to stand for what he believed.

Matt realized that these wicked people might win this round, but he also believed he will be used in the days of Armageddon to avenge their sinful souls.

Andrew was strapped down firmly. The executioner laughed at his new prey while he placed his hand on the decapitator lever. "Everyone, listen to me. Receive the Universal mark now or die like this." His fingers covered the death lever and he jerked it forcibly.

The blade flew downward.

Brandon saw the steel blade slice through Andrew's neck, beheading one of his best friends.

Andrew's decapitated head fell into a bucket, bounced out and rolled in a circle on the platform.

The executioner smiled at the opportunity to terrorize the crowd even further. Grabbing the head by its hair, he threw it at Brandon and Matt. "He was a friend of yours, huh?" As the bloody object sailed through the air, he continued, "Here's a gift for you."

Andrew's severed head flew straight at Brandon.

Brandon froze in his tracks, utterly stunned by the revelation. Matt didn't hesitate to help his friend and pushed Brandon out of the way. The gruesome head soared between them, spattering blood on them both.

Matt grabbed Brandon's arm in a firm grip. "Are you okay?"

Brandon trembled like a cold spell had attacked his body. Andrew's severed head lay a few feet away. He looked from the head and pointed an unsteady finger at his cheeks. "I can't lie, I'm petrified. Andrew's blood landed on my face."

Matt saw the splattered blood on Brandon, which caused anger to stir in his gut for these ill-spirited people. But his feelings could wait. The most important thing was to help his buddy to overcome his fears. He placed his hand on Brandon's shoulder and confessed, "I know, I'm scared too. But I truly believe my soul will be saved."

"I believe that too, but I'm so afraid! They cut off Andrew's head and threw it at us."

Matt shook Brandon's shoulders to gain his full attention. His next words were exceedingly important, and he had to make sure his

178

buddy understood them. "Don't be afraid! There is no fear in true love and that's what Jesus has for you. Do you want to see Lisa again?"

Bingo! That snapped Brandon back into focus. His head flinched as though a prizefighter had punched him. Once he heard the name, Lisa, his heart and soul leaped for joy.

The past few days have been so abusive, so much torment, it has thrown him into a tailspin. He basically didn't know up from down. But that was then and this is now! Brandon knew this was life or death, and he had two choices. Either receive the mark of the beast or have his head cut off.

He weighed the options, and he weighed them carefully.

If the Bible was true and he accepted the mark, he would condemn his soul straight to hellfire with no way out, just eternal damnation. He could walk now but his existence would be worthless. Plus he would never have the chance to see Lisa again.

Now came the other scenario.

If God's word was true, his body would die here but there will be something far greater in store for him: heaven, and possibly being with his lover.

Decision time, and it all came down to this question. Did he have enough faith in Christ Jesus to sacrifice his life in the hopes of something far greater?

When he was a child, someone once told him a couple important lessons about life. Always take personal responsibly for your actions and deeds, and this life was his choice so live it wisely. Always follow your heart, for it holds the answers. Then Matt's question exploded in his mind. "Do you want to see Lisa again?"

The thought brought tears to his eyes. "Yes, that's all I want. I want to be with Lisa again!"

Matt knew his time was approaching. "Then believe and be strong. Do not take the mark! Heaven is going to be so cool."

From nowhere, a guard jumped in front of them and crammed a cutoff head in front of Matt's face, shaking blood everywhere. "Are you ready to join us? Or die like this!"

Matt stared at the grisly object, wiped blood drops from his cheeks and told him, "Burn, demon, burn."

The guard became furious. "Kill this pecker-head! And kill him now."

Several officers grabbed Matt from the rear to force him towards the platform. But Matt started fighting and he was fighting hard, giving them a difficult time. He planted the heel of his boot harshly into a guard's shin that knocked the guard to the ground. Another officer was rushing over to help the others.

Once Matt saw his perfect chance, he executed a brutal front kick, nailing the officer between his legs. It threw the officer in the air at least a foot, and he plummeted to the dirt holding his crotch.

But a guard behind Matt was quick and slammed the stock of his machinegun against Matt's head. Matt staggered; his head was pounding uncontrollably. Five guards grabbed him and dragged him to the guillotine bed.

Brandon watched his best friend being strapped down. He wanted to help but couldn't. Two officers stood in front of him pointing shotguns at his head.

The moment they had Matt strapped down, the executioner snatched the handle. Matt knew what was happening, but found enough strength to yell at Brandon, "He that endureth unto the end, the same shall be saved!"

The blade soared down chopping off Matt's head. It fell into a bucket as streams of blood squirted from his severed neck, pulsating with every beat of his heart. Then his heart ceased to function and the stream fizzled to a drip.

Matt's body lay limp on the guillotine table, deceased.

The executioner was proud of his performance. "Grab the next one," he screamed devilishly.

Brandon felt caged in. His thoughts were clouded by the cold-blooded murder of his two best friends. He then saw three guards coming his way when another jumped in front of them, holding something behind his back. "You better join our club," he hollered as he crammed a bloody head in front of Brandon's face. "Or you'll be butchered!"

Brandon jumped back, shocked, and then noticed that the slaughtered head was Andrew's. "You son of a bitch," he yelled and lunged at the guard, not fearful to any degree. But two other officers slammed him to the ground.

Brandon crashed hard onto the dirt. Puffs of dust filled the air, but that didn't stop his will to fight or his longing to beat the evil. He immediately executed a sweeping sidekick and nailed a guard in the lower leg, dropping him to the dirt. Brandon jumped to his feet like a captured animal leaping from a cage. He had no concern for himself, just so long as he paid some of these bastards back.

Regrettably, he wasn't fast enough. An officer standing behind him smacked a wooden nightstick across his neck.

The blow knocked him to his knees. Brandon shook his head trying to regain his focus as four guards dragged him towards the platform. No time was given for him to catch his breath.

When they reached the table beside the staircase, Brandon fought them off. "Wait, hold on."

One of the head officers that wore a large pair of sunglasses approached. "Hold on, guys. Loosen the grip," he told his men. He looked into Brandon's eyes and saw fear but couldn't read him entirely. "Listen, boy. I'm trying to save your life. This is your last chance. Either join the Universal club and have freedom, or your head will be chopped off and you'll be dead like your friends."

Brandon's mind was reeling. A lot of confusion impacted his thoughts. He glanced at the table and then at the guillotine.

The officer smiled from thinking he had caught a new fish, another number to add on the list, and removed his sunglasses. This revealed the mark of the beast stamped on his forehead.

Brandon's full focus was pulled to the sinister stamp. It made his senses kick in and his fears were swept away. He yelled forcibly, "I pray the Lord will use me to avenge your evil souls. To hell with you and your devil mark!" Brandon punched the head officer in his face, bursting his nose that spewed blood everywhere.

As Brandon was cocking his arm back to strike again, several guards lunged at him. Then a guard jammed a cattle prodder into his side, zapping intense voltage throughout his body.

The electrical charge dropped Brandon to his knees.

Almost instantaneously, three guards dragged him up the stand and strapped him onto the guillotine table. The executioner grabbed the death lever.

Chapter 48

John the Disciple was busy writing everything in his scroll. He was having the time of his life being here, and then he saw seven angels flying to the altar. Each angel wore a white robe with a golden band wrapped around their chest, and they emitted pure power.

John gasped at their appearance. "It keeps getting better!"

The angel beside him chuckled. "Just wait, the best is yet to come. The final judgments of God shall now be delivered!"

John noticed that one of the four beasts that guarded the throne, the one with the head of a man, held a tray containing seven golden vials. The beast held the tray outwards, instructing the angels, "Take these vials."

As the golden vials were taken, God's voice rippled from the throne, "Go your ways and pour out the vials of my wrath upon the world."

The seven took off holding their golden vials in front, flying side by side into the sky. The first angel nodded at his partners and headed to an area in Northern Colorado.

# # #

In a wide-open field in the middle of nowhere, people were dancing near a huge concert stage. Hundreds of adults and kids were partying like they didn't have a care in the world. Many looked unwashed wearing psychedelic shirts while others wore very little.

It resembled closely to a Woodstock type of event except for one major difference.

On the stage where a band should be stood a forty-foot statue made in the image of the President, and it detailed his appearance perfectly. The Universal sign hung above the statue, pulsating hypnotically.

As it flashed, its bright light covered the crowd in a devilish red.

Several Universal guards walked through the crowd wearing T-shirts that had the <|> mark and the word "FREEBIES" printed on both sides. They also carried a square tin with the Universal mark stamped in dark print around it.

A guard named Matteo searched everywhere for his next victim. His car payment was due and he needed the extra commission the government paid to distribute the dope to the kids. But as the government phrased it: you are not pushing drugs, you are helping these people by giving them medicine.

Yeah, right. It might not be medicine but it was paying the bills, and that was all that mattered to Matteo. He noticed two teenagers coming into view and hurried their way before one of his coworkers reached them first.

The young adults sat on the grass. Matteo approached and thought he'd try the new routine the government taught him in a meeting last night. Act like you were stoned on dope. He swayed over, sat beside the couple and asked in his best drugged out voice, "How's it going, my friends?"

"It's okay. It sure is pretty out here," the girl replied pleasantly.

The softness in her voice brought joy to Matteo, she'll be an easy target, so he set the bait. "It sure is gorgeous. I just took some of this free medicine and I feel great! Would you like some?"

"That might be nice. Would you like a free tab?" the guy asked his girlfriend.

"Not me, I heard four people died from it last week."

"Aw, no! It wasn't from this," Matteo debated quickly. "They brought their own stuff and that's against the rules."

"Oh, I didn't know that," she stated. "If that's the case, then I'll try one."

"Okay, we'll take a couple tabs," her boyfriend agreed.

Matteo handed them two blue tablets. They took the pills and thanked him. Matteo stood. "Enjoy, man. If you folks want more." He hesitated for a few seconds to pretend like he was tripping. "Oh,

183

man. This stuff is good. If you want more my name is Matteo. Just look me up, I'll be somewhere."

He staggered away, chuckling, "Damn, they were right. If you act stoned these fools will trust you more. And that stupid bitch actually believed that someone brought their own stuff. Who's going to bring their own dope when they can get it for free? I hope she ODs today."

Matteo laughed wickedly as he saw several people on the stage praying to the statue. They were just a bunch of idiots. He could surly make some good money by pushing this crap on them.

Heading their way, Matteo didn't bother with a couple that was lying behind the bushes a few feet away. There were many more fish on the stage to fry.

Behind the shrubs, a teenage couple was making out heavily on a cheap blanket, groping the others body.

# # #

The first vial angel sailed over the field like a jet fighter heading into combat. The instant he saw the people worshipping the false idol, he sneered in disgust and held his golden cup high in the air.

Tipping the vial on its side, dark red liquid poured over the beveled edge and spilled to the earth. Then the warrior of God headed back to heaven, vanishing into the clouds.

The first angel poured out his vial upon the earth; and there fell a noisome and grievous sore upon the men which had the mark of the beast, and upon them that worshipped his image.
Revelation 16:2

# # #

Behind the bushes, the teenagers were kissing lustfully. The guy was cramming his tongue down her mouth as a gust of wind blew his hair over his eyes. The girl backed off slightly and brushed his hair to the side, which exposed the mark stamped on his forehead, the same mark stamped on her right hand.

He positioned his body over hers while whispering in her ear, "Get ready, baby. I'm about to rock your world!"

The girl's eyes were clinched, longing. She heard her boyfriend moan and this made her gasp in anticipation. She then felt an unusual sensation overcome her.

Before she concluded what it was, lover boy rolled off her, squealing, "Ouch, my face is on fire!" He wailed loudly while rubbing his head with both hands.

The girl became totally confused. She pulled his fingers from his head which revealed a repulsive sight. The boy's face was covered in gory welts with blisters oozing pus.

She screamed wildly as she yanked his hands down even further, causing pus to seep from his face to his hands like spaghetti was hanging between them.

The girl yelled hysterically and ran away, leaving the boy grieving in pain.

#   #   #

It was a dark evening in a condemned building in downtown Chicago. Graffiti covered the walls. Three skinny drug addicts were huddled on the floor trying to light a candle with shaky hands.

Rusty pulled a bag of black tar heroin out of his pocket. Once he opened the wrapper, the scent of the drug filled the air.

Melvin shouted, "Hurry up, man. Cook that stuff."

"Shut up. How am I going to cook it when you haven't lit the candle?"

"It'll be lit in a minute." Melvin looked at their other friend. "Come on, buggerhead, and light the candle."

"Quit calling me buggerhead. My name is Billy!" he declared while holding a match to the candle's wick. It sparked to life, delivering light into the environment.

"That's right. Billy the buggerhead," Melvin teased. He immediately threw his attention back to Rusty who was placing a burnt spoon over the candle.

Drool formed in Melvin's mouth as he watched the heroin sizzle. "Man, you take too long."

"Shut up and strap your arm," Rusty snapped back.

Melvin turned to Billy and laughed. Billy was picking his nose with his right hand that had the mark stamped.

"Hey buggerhead, it looks like you're trying to sniff that mark off your hand."

Billy pulled his hand down. "I ain't doing nothing."

"Yeah, right." Melvin tossed him the strap. "Here you go, strap me up. And make sure you don't have any buggers on your hands, you buggerhead."

"Shut up," Billy demanded while he tied the strap around Melvin's arm.

A few feet away Rusty was pumping the syringe with a large hit of heroin.

When Melvin's arm was tied, he placed it in front of Rusty and begged like a child asking for candy, "Here you go, my friend. Fill me up."

As Rusty positioned the needle flawlessly above the vein, the gruesome sores blossomed on Melvin's arm, covering them entirely. His flesh turned into jelly, causing the needle to slip away.

Melvin screamed painfully, "What are you doing to my arm?"

"I ain't done anything," Rusty confessed. "Look at your arm, it's gross!"

Melvin cried, "What is it? It burns like fire!"

Rusty stared at him and then his head was knocked back like someone had punched him. Rusty rubbed his face, hollering excruciatingly. One side of his head was covered in sores. He pulled his hands down. Slimy pus was sticking between them. "Ugh, what is this crap?" Then his head was knocked back again with sores coating both sides of his face.

Billy the buggerhead freaked. "What the hell's happening? I'm getting out of here." He backstroked across the floor with everything he had.

But there was no escape. This was God's prophecy being fulfilled.

Billy's head was slammed backwards as sores engulfed his face. Intense pain attacked his nervous system to the point of where he collapsed flat on the floor, shaking like a leaf.

Chapter 49

Brandon soared rapidly through a tunnel of light and landed on soft ground. What just happened? Beauty thrived around him like he had never imagined, even in his most pleasant dreams. "Oh, my. This must be heaven. It's awesome," he gasped, and then wondered how he could see again after losing his head. He was beheaded only seconds before.

He threw his hands to his head and was astonished.

It was now there! His body was whole again. How could this be? Brandon glanced to his side and saw Matt standing beside him.

A wholesome grin covered Matt's face as he laughed enthusiastically. "Hello, buddy. Welcome to paradise!"

Brandon's mouth dropped. "Matt, what's happening? Your head is on your body. But I saw them cut it off."

"Yeah, your head is there, too. You're in heaven, everyone is complete here. I knew those fools could hurt us for only a short period. And look around, isn't this place cool?"

Fascination flourished in Brandon's eyes. The colors that surrounded him were breathtaking. "This is fine!" Someone called his name. Brandon turned and saw another terrific sight. "Tommy, Andrew, everyone is here." Now Lisa dominated his thoughts, and he asked hopefully, "Has anyone seen Lisa? Has anyone seen my baby?"

Matt shook his head. "Not yet, we just got here so give it some time. All things are possible, especially when you're here."

"Yeah, my friend. Keep your head up now that you have one again," Andrew joked. Everyone laughed. Andrew noticed something very special. "Oh, my gosh! There are my parents. They died over ten years ago. I can't wait to see them. Come on, Tommy,

188

let's go." Andrew and Tommy took off. Tommy yelled in mid-stride, "Hello, Mr. and Ms. Beckinsale."

The moment Andrew's parents saw them, their faces blossomed in happiness. Andrew hugged them warmly as Tommy joined in with a group hug.

Brandon and Matt smiled. "That's nice," Brandon remarked.

Matt gestured. "Yeah it is, and check it out. Since I arrived a few minutes before you, I had a chance to look around."

Brandon scanned the area in amazement. Pastures and waterfalls were flowing abundantly to his right, and a city of lights that reached to the sky was on his left. But mainly he was searching for only one thing: Lisa. He spotted several pure white horses grazing in an open field.

A large stallion stared at Brandon and snorted in friendship. "Look at that pretty horse, Matt. I think he likes me." The stallion suddenly lifted off the ground and flew toward him. "Check it out. They can fly!" Brandon shrieked.

# # #

The six vial angels cruised in unison like the Blue Angels Air Force team. After a short distance, the two on the end split from the group and went into different directions.

The second angel sailed to the blue waters of the Pacific Ocean. Slowing to a stop above the rippling waves, he dipped his finger in the sea and tasted the salt water.

Then the warrior of God poured his vial into the sea, which turned the ocean into blood. And this blood smelt of rotting death. The angel flew back into the sky leaving the judgment to do its duty.

Almost instantly, redness devoured every ocean worldwide, killing every creature that lived in the sea.

The second angel poured out his vial upon the sea; and it became
as the blood of a dead man: and every living creature died in the
sea.
Revelation 16:3
189

The President was stomping down the hallway with anger fuming through his veins. Passing his secretary, he didn't acknowledge her as he stormed into the Oval Office. He immediately spotted Smitty sitting in his regular spot, his plush leather chair. "What are you doing here?"

Smitty looked him at confusingly. "What do you mean? I'm here for our one-o'clock lunch date."

"Lunch date," Jeff crowed. "So what are you, my bitch?"

"You'd be so lucky if I was," Smitty shot back jokingly. "But to be serious, we have reservations at MaPlage, and the food there is simply delicious."

"Simply delicious, huh?" the President mocked. "Didn't you hear about the nasty sores that attacked many of our followers?"

"Of course I heard about it. But to use your term, they're just collateral damage."

Jeff laughed out loud. "Now you're sounding like me! And since you hear about everything, what the hell is coming next?"

"I wish I knew that answer because things are coming at us quickly."

There was a knock on the office door, then it opened slightly. The President's secretary poked her head in. "Excuse me, gentlemen. Father Smitty, as you requested, your America Today paper just arrived. Would you like it now?"

"That's great, thank you Jessica." She stepped in the Oval Office and handed him the paper, then lowered her head and exited while closing the door behind her. Smitty opened the paper and his eyes were instantly pulled to the main article on the front page. As he studied it, he mumbled, "Oh, my. This isn't good."

Jeff noticed Smitty's concern. "What are you talking about?"

Smitty shook his head as he closed the paper. "Oh, it's nothing," he responded while trying to hide his true emotions. He didn't care to be the one to show this to Jeff.

But Jeff sensed the lie. "Don't you lie to me, boy. Now tell me what's in that paper!"

"Here you go, read it yourself." Smitty rolled the paper and tossed it to Jeff, who caught it in midair. As he looked at the front page, his face soured. "These stinking pieces of crap! How dare they call me the 'Devil President'! If they think I'm evil by chopping off a few stinking heads, then they haven't seen shit!" He threw the paper on the floor. It landed face up, showing the main article – a picture of a blood-splashed guillotine with the headline:

The Beheading of Innocent Americans.
Is Jeff Christensen the Devil President?

Right as Jeff stormed to his desk, the phone rang. He yanked the receiver and spoke in a low graveled voice, "Who is it and what do they want?"

His secretary could hear the tension in his voice. "Mr. President, it's the Secretary of State on line one. Should I transfer the call?"

"Go ahead," he responded and the call was connected. The Secretary of State stated, "Mr. President, there is a problem. Somehow the oceans worldwide have been turned into blood and our scientists are completely baffled as to why."

Jeff yelled into the receiver, "Then fire those idiot scientists and hire ones who know what they're doing! And do it now!" He slammed the phone down and stared at Smitty. "This sucks!"

Chapter 50

In an untouched environment in the mountains of Oregon, a fresh water spring flowed lavishly through the terrain. Flowers blossomed in lush bushes, delivering the smell of nature. During this part of the tribulation not many clean areas existed. Especially after so many plagues have devoured the earth.

But this place was unique.

Redken the hunter was crouched at the edge of the creek. Dressed entirely in military fatigues, he blended in superbly. Even animals would have trouble separating him from the bush.

A sinister glare beamed in his eyes as Redken rubbed dirt from his forehead, revealing the mark <|> stamped permanently above his eyebrows. He began to move closer to the creek.

The water should attract many animals, and he hungered to butcher every one of them.

As he approached the stream, he couldn't believe the sight. The water looked clear. Could the stream actually have clean water?

Without delay, the hunter crawled on the ground like a snake slithering across the dirt. Once he reached the creek, he stuck his head over the edge and licked the water. "It's fresh water!" he yelled joyfully.

Redken felt like the most fortunate person in the world. He hasn't had luck of this magnitude in some time. Well, he did have a good streak seven days ago.

Recalling the events of a week ago in another part of the woods, Redken snuck up on a pair of hunters who were discussing that they were down to their last two canteens of spring water. One hunter laughed at how much they could sell the water for. His partner responded it didn't matter. They were worth millions simply because the full canteens could keep them alive for a few days.

The men were so involved in their conversation they never heard Redken stalking in the woods.

Right when they were about to take a sip of the life saving water, Redken took his cue. "Hello, fellow campers. May I enter your campground?"

The hunters glanced at each other, then stared at him. The approaching stranger looked pleasant enough. His hair was trimmed clean and he wore the more expensive camouflaged hunting attire. His rifle alone must have cost over two thousand dollars. Against their better judgment, they allowed him to join.

Then again, they should have known that appearances could be deceiving.

Redken approached with a warm smile, a caring smile. "Guys, I'm about to die of thirst. I accidentally heard that you have some spring water. Can I have a taste of that water?"

"I'm sorry but there is so little," one hunter replied. "Maybe we can spare a small drink to help you get by."

That wasn't the answer that Redken wanted. The hell with just a sip, he wanted more. Redken wanted it all. "Yeah, I understand. You are sorry."

In a quick move, Redken raised his rifle and shot the guy in the face, exploding the camper's head into a pink mist. Brains splattered in the air while his body was thrown to the hard dirt.

Just as the other camper grasped what took place, Redken flung his hunting knife in a spiral motion into the man's chest, stabbing him through his lungs.

Redken walked over, noticed that the person was still alive, just barely gasping for air, and yanked the knife from the camper's chest. Then Redken unconscientiously sliced it across the man's throat, basically chopping the camper's head from his body. It was dangling only by a few strands of bloody tissue.

Redken smiled at the killing as he wiped the stained blade across the dead person's clothes. He surely didn't want to get his own outfit dirty.

Laughing aloud, he picked up the two canteens and crowed, "That's what you get for not giving me what I wanted. Now I'll give you a small drink of my water." He rinsed out his mouth and spit the backwash in their faces.

Redken snapped out of the trance as a large smile beamed on his face. Pleasurable memories always made his heart happy. Except his current situation was even better than killing those two greedy hunters. Fresh spring water was flowing beneath him.

He jumped in the water and splashed it over his face, drinking several handfuls.

# # #

The third vial angel flew toward the snow peaked Cascade Ranges and sailed over a large river as the crystal clear water flowed beneath him.

The angel came to a sudden stop above the reservoir, poured the thick liquid from his vial into the water, and the river turned into a puddle of blood.

The warrior cruised back to heaven while the streams and lakes turned red.

***The third angel poured out his vial upon the rivers and fountains
of waters; and they became blood.
Revelation 16:4***

# # #

Redken was having a splendid time splashing in the spring water, but there were more important things to do. He needed to fill the canteens that he stole from the dead men.

The spring water's radiant appearance caused a tingling sensation to surge in his body. "Fresh water, yeah man. There's going to be a lot of animals for me to kill, and I can't wait to butcher every one of them and eat their juicy flesh."

The canteens filled so he secured the caps and placed them in his belt. Unable to resist another taste of fresh water, he dipped his hands in the stream. He had to take advantage of this opportunity while it lasted.

194

Dousing water over his head, Redken tried to wash away his human scent. This way the animals couldn't detect him. But while he rinsed his face, the blood stream flowed his way like a killer stalking its prey.

He took another drink and purred affectionately, "This tastes so good I think it's time to slaughter some animals. My belly is getting hungry for fresh meat. But one last sip can't hurt anything."

As the hunter placed his face in the water, his destiny had arrived. The blood stream coated him, changing the surroundings from tranquil into pure gore.

Redken felt the density of water suddenly thicken so he pulled his head out of the horrid liquid. With a sour expression consuming his face, he spit out a mouthful of blood, squirting it between his teeth, and saw that he was covered and standing in a creek of it.

Redken screamed in horror as his feet began to shuffle beneath him. But he stumbled over a slippery stone and tumbled backwards, splashing into the death liquid.

Directly where his head was landing, a sharp rock was sticking out of the stream and stabbed him brutally in the back of his head, which poked his eyes outward like his brain had imploded from the inside out.

Blood flowed over his body, swallowing him forever, delivering no mercy to Redken's ungodly soul.

# # #

Inside a laboratory, several scientists studied a live magnified image of the earth from the Hubble telescope. The sight fascinated them. The world looked entirely different than it had just days before.

There was only blood and land, fresh or saltwater had become nonexistent.

A new sight appeared. A sight that shocked them even worse than the blood water. A gigantic angel was soaring to the earth in an incredible speed.

Many of the scientists shook their head confusingly. How could this be? They were watching something that they have argued for

195

years that didn't exist, and this completely destroyed their liberal theology.

The angel came to a stop above the plasmatic sea. "Thou art righteous, O Lord, because thou hast judged them. For they have shed the blood of saints and prophets and thou hast given them blood to drink; for they are worthy."

He glanced over the ocean with the knowledge that this was blood for blood.

The angel smiled and flew back to the Kingdom of God.

Chapter 51

In the lush green pastures of paradise, the beautiful white stallion captivated Brandon. The horse flew straight at him and landed on the ground. Then it rubbed his head gently against Brandon's arm.

Brandon instinctively reached out to pet the animal. "Look how tame he is."

Another horse flew down and landed in front of Matt. Matt stared at him, surprised by the swiftness of the creature. "Hey, I think this one likes me."

Brandon's curiosity overcame him. "I wonder if they'll let us ride them?"

"There's only one way to find out. Come on, let's give it a try."

Brandon and Matt didn't waste a moment. They walked beside the horses and hopped on with ease. The animals lifted their heads, snorted jubilantly, then took off into the air.

Brandon held on for dear life. He was flying far faster than any automobile could ever produce. While cruising through the sky, he noticed that he was hundreds of feet above the ground. Panic smacked him. What would happen if he fell off and plummeted downwards?

That thought quickly vanished when he discovered that he fit the horse perfectly, as though it had been custom tailored for his body.

They sailed in the sky, gliding effortlessly. Brandon smiled at Matt. It was all so remarkable.

Matt's eyes glowed of true happiness.

Their horses suddenly slowed to a stop as a mighty angel on horseback flew down. "Are you Brandon and you are named Matt?"

They both nodded yes.

"Come with me, you have been summoned," the angel commanded. His horse turned and flew away as hastily as it had arrived.

Brandon looked at Matt, Matt stared back, both wondering if they had done something wrong. Before they knew the answer, their horses took off to follow the angel, leaving them absolutely no control of the situation. They were in for the ride if they wished to be or not.

# # #

Circling the earth's atmosphere, the four vial angels were waiting for their turn to do their duty. The fourth angel took off by himself to Los Angeles.

Swooping down from the sky, he landed above the Hollywood sign in a cloud of dust. He was searching for one house in particular and to his delight he saw it perched on top of the next ridge.

Up in heaven the angels were able to see all things as they manifested and there was a person who caught his attention. A person who was worthy to receive major punishment.

The fourth vial angel decided to fly over Hollywood Boulevard. As he sailed over the famous street, he thought about his mission and knew this story had enough power to win a golden award. For many dreams will say so.

Chapter 52

A bright sun beamed in the sky, turning this into a perfect day for a backyard pool party. Fat cop Joe had the whole gang at his house. Surprisingly, he had a gorgeous place in the Hollywood Hills that had a fabulous view of Los Angeles.

His three police buddies, Frank, Yurik and Peter, along with four females, were having fun by a swimming pool.

Joe had a new woman he was trying to impress. Stepping out of the pool, he shook water from his thinning hair and grabbed a towel. The song on the radio ended.

"What an afternoon!" a fast talking D.J. spoke. "Can you believe this weather? It's a 104° out there, my little kitty cats. It's so hot we should all find a cool corner to cuddle up in. But while you're looking for that corner, I think it's time to get down with some disco. And as hot as it is, it's time to Burn, Baby Burn. Yes, my little kitty cats, it's Disco Inferno time!"

The music played loudly. Joe started to dance, moving his fat butt from side to side, causing everyone to laugh joyfully. They sang along and Joe really acted like a fool, shaking everything he had. "Burn, baby burn. Disco Inferno."

He jumped around energetically and straddled the towel between his legs like a stripper on stage. Kicking his feet forward, Joe humped the towel like a sex object. Everyone sang along.

# # #

While hovering in the sky, the fourth vial angel watched Joe make an idiot of himself. "So you like the song; Burn, baby burn. Disco Inferno? Watch this."

He took off into space, stopped halfway between the earth and sun, and poured out his vial. As it flowed to the sun, he commanded, "Burn. Baby burn." The instant the red liquid touched the sun, it brightened a thousand times in intensity.

A massive fireball exploded outwards, consuming the angel. But he soared through the fire and flew happily back to heaven.

The fourth angel poured out his vial upon the sun; and power was given unto it to scorch men with fire.
Revelation 16:8

#   #   #

Joe boogied beside his girlfriend as temptingly as possible. His expression reflected sinfulness. He couldn't wait to bang this chick.

Fat cop Joe wanted to make her scream with pleasure. Licking his fingertip, he rubbed it over the mark stamped on her forehead, the same mark as on his.

He swayed his hips to the side, threw the towel behind her head and pulled her close. "What do you think about big Joe now?"

"Nobody can make it burn like you, big Joe," she giggled, but she might have spoken too soon. The sun came blazing down, piercing the earth's atmosphere.

Joe's girlfriend pushed him away. "What's happening? It's getting too hot!"

Yurik caught on to the situation. He bolted out of his chair, glanced over Los Angeles and witnessed a spellbinding sight. The sun's blinding heat was bleaching the city.

Right below Joe's wooden deck, where the hills supported its foundation, several dry bushes sparked into flames under the sun's magnified force.

Yurik was puzzled to what was happening. He hoped it wasn't another judgment. After witnessing a fellow comrade get tortured by the evil locusts, he had become confused to whether there might be a higher being or not.

200

Could there be a God that created everything? A God that could actually save your soul and put you in heaven?

Yurik tried to learn the answer and asked several of his comrades, but by their responses he realized there couldn't. One way to justify this was a person like Joe. If there were a God then why would he put someone like Joe here?

With Yurik's eyes still closed to the truth, a burst of searing hot rays blasted down on him. "I hope it's not another plague from God," he screamed and swatted at his face like bees were buzzing around it.

Joe was quick to respond. He cursed, "There ain't no God! And to hell with him if there is!" The instant he spoke those words, the sun intensified massively. The little patch of hair on Joe's half balding scalp went up into a puff of smoke. He screamed painfully as he smacked the top of his head, but it didn't help.

Panicked, Joe looked everywhere and spotted the coolness of the pool water. He took off in a fast dash, yelling in mid-stride, "Everybody, the pool. The water will protect us."

Fat cop Joe dove in first that splashed water over the concrete edges. Everybody followed and jumped in behind him. The large body of water brought soothing relief.

Joe leaped out of the water, beaming, "I told you the pool will protect us."

His girlfriend threw her arms around his fat waist. "How could I ever doubt you?"

Joe reached behind her and pinched her butt. "I don't know, baby. Don't you know that big Joe is the baddest there is!"

"Oh, big Joe, you are bad," the dimwit asserted. She could feel her senses twinge in sexual excitement. Her body was becoming hotter. She then realized it wasn't Joe that was heating her up - it was the water.

Even though the water had given them a brief relief from the blistering heat, it was only temporary. Intense rays blazed to the earth that turned the pool water into a boiling hell.

The girl hollered in pain, "The water is burning me alive!"

Joe's fat arm splashed down producing a hot wave of scalding water that doused into her mouth, scorching her throat. She gasped painfully as she was swept under the sweltering water.

Joe bounced up and down, spinning about. His face was turning bright red while he cried out in agony, "Screw you, God! We will win."

Immediately following his outburst, Joe was sucked under the boiling mist. Hot turbulence churned that threw him back and forth like a great white shark was attacking him.

Joe was then tossed out of the pool and landed on the concrete ledge, resembling a beached whale that had invaded the shoreline.

But a change was taking place. Joe's body swelled to double its original size. Blisters and welts were flourishing over every inch of his flesh.

As Yurik was boiling to death, he wondered why such torturous judgments were being inflicted upon the world. But subconsciously he knew it was because people were non-repentant of their sinful deeds. Disbelief and coldness of heart were the reasons for the ten plagues against Pharaoh and the great city Egypt in the days of Moses. The only difference was, Yurik knew the end was near. But he had made his choice in life.

Scorching waters whipped the group about the pool, slamming them from one side of the concrete structure to the other. They tried desperately to escape this torment but the boiling waters sucked their bodies under the bubbly mist. Their eternal hell was just beginning.

And men were scorched with great heat and blasphemed the name of God, which hath power over these plagues: and they repented not to give him glory.
Revelation 16:9

Chapter 53

With three vial angels left, they thundered through the sky side by side. The fifth smiled happily as he poured the liquid from his golden cup.

Something strange began to happen.

The brightness that surrounded them grew extremely dark, and then evil faces flashed abruptly towards them, trying to attack the celestial beings. The hideous souls were screeching agonizingly as torment filled their existence, but they were no match for the angels.

The fifth angel wanted to have more fun so he smacked his golden vial across a demon's head, knocking the degenerate backwards.

The evil soul wailed in pain while he was sucked through a time warp into the fiery pits of hell.

Then a large fireball flashed at the angels consuming them in blistering flames. But they breached it triumphantly as smoke streamed behind them like a tornado raging in the air.

The fifth angel took off by himself.

The fifth angel poured out his vial upon the throne of the beast; and his kingdom was full of darkness; and they gnawed their tongues for pain, and blasphemed the God of heaven because of their pains and their sores, and repented not of their deeds.
Revelation 16:10,11

Only the sixth and seventh vial angels remained. With the ultimate battle looming in the near future, the sixth vial angel waved at his partner and flew to the earth. He was headed to Baghdad and the Euphrates river.

Flying at an immense speed, he sailed over the Euphrates and poured the liquid from his golden cup.

As it splashed into the river, it dried up. Even the wet dirt that surrounded the riverbank dried into dust, preparing the pathway for war.

The sixth angel poured out his vial upon the great river Euphrates; and the water thereof was dried up, that the way of the kings of the east might be prepared. And the beast gathered them together into a place called in the Hebrew tongue ARMAGEDDON.
Revelation 16:12,16

Chapter 54

Inside the Oval Office, Jeff Christensen was pacing back and forth. He had to figure his next countermove. A new employee, a young scholar named Howard, sat at a large table studying the Bible.

Jack Smitty sat at the other side of the table looking at a map of Jerusalem.

The President yelled at the scholar, "What does that book say? What's going to happen next?"

Howard shrugged his shoulders. He didn't have an intelligent answer. "I'm not sure. I always studied the Old Testament, not the New. A lot of this is foreign to me."

"What did you say?" Jeff exploded. "You stupid idiot. I give you a job to interpret that book and you don't know jack about it. You're screwed up, that's what you are!" The President slapped him brutally across his head, knocking it forward.

Howard held his head down in pain but also because he was afraid of Jeff Christensen. There was something about that man that scared him badly.

Luckily for Howard the phone rang that pulled Jeff's attention. He stomped to it and yanked the receiver from its cradle. "What! Yeah, put him on."

His tone lowered. "Hello, Sam. This is the President. What do you have for me?" Jeff's face soured. "When did this happen?" He hung up and stated in pure anger, "Every damn ocean and lake worldwide has been turned into blood! And the great Euphrates river has been dried into dust."

"Oh, shit!" Smitty reacted. "Our armies will die soon if the water has been turned into blood."

The remark infuriated Jeff. "Don't you think I know that? You fool!" Jeff yelled at the scholar, "Hey, you. What's that book say about this?"

The scholar spoke softly while staring in the Bible, "I made such a mistake by not believing this. It's so clear to me now." He noticed Jeff coming his way and spoke up, "It's not good, sir. According to the Book of Revelation, the sixth vial has been poured and that means the end is near."

The President became fully enraged. Fire was burning in his eyes. "What the hell did you say? The end is near? That's bullshit!" Jeff grabbed Howard's Bible and threw it across the room. Its pages fanned open like a dove as it sailed in the air, then the book smashed against the wall and fell forcibly to the ground.

Jeff pointed at heaven and screamed, "I don't care what that Bible says. Damn that God and his word! I am the antichrist, my father's son, and I'm going to slaughter God and his army of angels once and for all!"

Jeff's face wrinkled as he hissed at Smitty, "This is it! We're going to Jerusalem. It's time for the killing!"

He opened his mouth in blasphemy against God, to blaspheme his name, and his tabernacle, and them that dwell in heaven.
Revelation 13:6

Chapter 55

Soaring temperatures were peaking around 120-degrees in the desert outside of Baghdad. The ground was trembling as a huge amount of military equipment: tanks, Hummers, halftracks, along with thousands upon thousands of soldiers moved across the desert. They were traveling to the hill country of Megiddo and the valley of Esdraelon, approximately fifty miles north of Jerusalem, the prophesied area of Armageddon.

A soldier wiped sweat from his forehead and looked at the sky. An F-16 fighter jet flew above him in the cloudy and overcast day.

At the front of the pack, a large battle tank bumped along with the lead general sitting halfway out of the turret. It gave him such a rush to have the tank rumbling so gracefully beneath his body. He pointed his finger forward while his eyes showed he was ready to give it all to win this war.

The general recalled a meeting he had with the President where he was warned that this battle could be extreme. But he didn't care: the more excessive, the better.

Wind thrashed over the desert which blasted a handful of sand into his face. He coughed severely, spit it out and cursed the dirt. Why did they have to fight this battle in the hot ass barren desert?

But then the general noticed something unusual happening above.

The sky was growing extremely dark, like the clouds were tumbling from the inside out. The general reached his arm to the sky trying to touch them, but knew he couldn't. So he commanded his soldiers to progress onward.

# # #

The seventh vial angel hovered in the earth's atmosphere as he surveyed the soldiers with a magnified vision. He found it difficult to believe that the evil ones could deceive so many humans. The damnation their souls would soon endure.

Wind blew vigorously across the angel's face. He couldn't wait to revenge those who have come to make war against God and the warrior angels, so he poured out his golden vial into the air.

The liquid flowed toward the soldiers, spreading out like a spider web. The ultimate battle between good and evil was quickly approaching.

The seventh angel poured out his vial into the air; and there came a great voice out of the temple of heaven, from the throne, saying, It is done.
Revelation 16:17

Chapter 56

In the middle of the desert, dust covered the soldiers in murky grime. The general looked over the wasteland and was furious that his enemies were nowhere to be found. When he spoke to the President about the battle plans, he was told that his opponents could pop out of nowhere, but he laughed it off.

The general noticed the clouds turning darker, almost to the point of being pitch black, and it upset him tremendously. "Get out of here so I can find my enemies and kill them!"

At that very second, hundreds of lightning bolts flashed, thundering intensely. The clouds started to swirl in a circular motion, spinning robustly, and were sucked into the sky as though they were never there.

The sun sparked to life, delivering a pathway of brightness to the army. The general snarled, "What the hell?"

As every eye focused above, the prophecy of all times was revealed.

Jesus Christ appeared sitting on his pure white stallion. His hair and robe was flowing in the breeze, exposing a sight for all to behold.

His massive army of angels, the warriors of heaven, covered the sky behind him completely dominating the horizon.

The angels wore long white jackets and sat boldly on their white horses. They resembled a pack of renegade cowboys ready to rock the world!

The image of Jesus was majestic as it was with John at Patmos. His eyes flamed of fire. A golden crown sat on his head. A long white robe was draped over his shoulders that flowed over the horse.

His warrior angels filled the sky going back as far as the eye could see.

His top angel, Eric, the preacher man from Lisa's dream, hovered in the air beside him. And beside Eric were two familiar faces, Brandon and Matt, who were now warriors in God's army. Jesus nodded to let them know the time for battle was near.

Every angel held a chromed sword that was unique in many ways. Eric held his sword outward while he looked at the masses of infidel soldiers who have come to make war against them.

Jesus knew his angels have been waiting for this moment. He instructed one that held a golden trumpet, "The time is at hand, blow thy trumpet." The angel blew the horn powerfully.

The trumpet blast echoed over the world as Jesus' voice thundered, "Go!"

Eric smiled in anticipation from yearning for this day. This was the time to destroy everyone who had chosen corruption. This was the ultimate confrontation - God and his army of angels against the devil and his.

The Judgment was finally here. This was The Second Coming!

Eric held his sword high as he screamed to attack. His stallion raced in the sky, snorting vigorously, and the army of angels traveled fiercely to the earth.

I saw heaven opened, and behold a white horse; and he that sat upon him was called Faithful and True, and in righteousness he doth judge and make war. And the armies which were in heaven followed him upon white horses, clothed in fine linen, white and clean.
Revelation 19:11,14

# # #

Dust covered the soldiers and military equipment from every part of the world. Satan had truly used his power to bring this mass together. As every person stared upwards in astonishment, the expression on the general's face said it all. The sky was full of attacking angels on horseback descending rapidly upon his army.

The blazing sun shone vibrantly on the angel's chromed swords, which lit the sky in millions of sparkling blades. And the blades grew in size as they arrived closer.

The lifelong military general gawked at what could be sure death. "Aw, shit!" he howled. "Look at the size of that army! How can we defeat them?"

# # #

Leading the warriors downward, Eric searched his enemies to find his first target. His horse was also giving everything it had to charge at the soldiers. Even the animal wanted a piece of the evil ones.

Eric saw exactly what he hoped for, the leader of their pack.

The general was sitting halfway out of the tank's turret, commanding, "Attack, shoot. Kill'em, kill'em all!"

His entire army let go with everything they had. Tanks, cannons, and thousands of soldiers were shooting randomly into the sky. They were trying to hit something, anything. Angels were everywhere.

Bombs exploded in the sky near the angels but it didn't affect them. They were virtually unfazed by the human weapons. A bomb blew up in front of Eric's face that threw spent gunpowder and shrapnel around him. He shook his head and sailed through the debris as he headed for the general who was still barking attack orders.

Eric knew the general should die first. He sped toward him in lightning speed, like a burst of wind whipping in the air.

The general's eyes grew in size when he saw the huge horse and rider approaching. In a fast move, he shot several rounds from his pistol but Eric blocked the bullets with his sword. One after another, the bullets weren't able to penetrate the angel's domain.

Eric kicked his heels on the horse to push him further, but there was no need. The horse was just as thrilled as he.

Arriving closer to the general, Eric swung his shiny piece of steel and sliced the general's body in half. The upper part of the general's torso toppled over the tank, dowsing the metal in blood at every location it hit. Then his upper torso slammed onto the ground and landed upwards, appearing to be buried halfway in the dirt.

Eric rushed onward into battle. Matt was directly behind him.

Matt saw the general's half torso. Swooping down, he pushed a special button on his sword that made a pitchfork pop out. He then speared the general's back like a fish and flew over the soldiers holding the wretched half body out for all to see.

In the foreground, Matt noticed a soldier pointing a gun at him. That would be the last mistake that person ever made. Matt rushed over and smacked the soldier with the gory torso, knocking him to his knees.

Matt flew away chuckling at how swiftly he concocted these cleaver war maneuvers. He kept sailing above the soldiers while he beat them with the general's bloody torso.

Brandon flew past Matt and he was ready to take care of business. Back in his childhood he used to play with little toy soldiers and toy tanks, so now he wanted to play with the real ones.

Brandon noticed a tank in the foreground and dive-bombed it viciously. In mid-stride, he threw his sword at the metal vehicle.

The navigator inside tank glanced out of the peephole to an unexpected sight. The shiny steel blade of the sword was heading straight at him. Piercing the glass peephole, it nailed him directly between his eyes, right below the mark of the beast stamped on his forehead. The pressure of the harpooning sword plummeted him backwards into the driver that sat behind him, spearing them both together. Dying helplessly beside each other, they never knew it would be like this.

Just as Brandon grabbed another sword from his side, an F-16 fighter jet soared past him in a low swooping pass. The pilot was gunning the jet in the attempts of running over a few angels; they filled the sky in every direction.

As the pilot grabbed the fighter stick, a feeling of false supremacy consumed his body. Laughing demonically, he positioned the weapon of destruction and squeezed the trigger so tightly his knuckles were turning a bright shade of white.

The steel barrels of the 20mm Vulcan twisted in a circular motion, firing bullets at the rate and power that could level a baseball stadium in seconds flat.

Brandon and three other angels dodged the oncoming lead and teamed-up to dive-bomb the jet. They threw their swords at the cockpit of the aircraft.

Once the pilot saw the shiny objects sailing at him, he wailed fearfully. Then the swords burst through the hardened glass and speared him ruthlessly from his neck to his groin. The extreme pressure against his body slammed his hand against the joystick, which plunged the jet to the ground where it exploded into a fireball. Burning gasoline splashed over many soldiers, scorching them to death.

Brandon flew on to find his partners.

Chapter 57

The battle of Armageddon surged on as Eric and his stallion raced toward a large group of soldiers. Brandon and Matt joined in beside him and they formed a pyramid, a fighting force to be reckoned with.

Brandon loved the excitement. Ever since his beheading this experience has been absolutely amazing. Eric was directly in front of him charging at several soldiers who were firing machineguns their way. Bullets were zipping everywhere.

Once Eric arrived closer to them, he cocked his sword back and brutally beheaded three soldiers. Their heads plopped to the dirt as blood squirted from their bodies into the sky like a bloody fountain, and their torsos collapsed to the ground.

Brandon's horse flew forward while weapons fired abundantly. He noticed danger ahead. His instinct told him to do battle, but he was a lover, not a fighter. Then a bullet smacked him on his shoulder that twisted him sideways in the saddle. He stared at the wound in total shock, but somehow it healed miraculously before his very eyes. He couldn't believe how rapidly his body had regenerated!

Brandon looked up and spotted another soldier pointing a weapon at him. The image startled him, making him freeze. But Eric flew in and chopped off the soldier's head, saving Brandon from any potential harm.

Eric pointed his finger at Brandon to tell him to get with the program.

After Brandon saw the intensity in Eric, he remembered that this was Armageddon, the war against evil. This was the time to destroy all whom had chosen the devil over God. The people they were fighting would gladly kill him, his family, and even Lisa.

Right as that thought impacted him, Brandon held the sword tightly in his hand as bullets whizzed by his face. He gripped the horse's reins, kicked his feet on the animal's side and in his mind the battle was on!

Brandon flew at a soldier seeking Sweet Revenge. Closing in, he reared his sword and sliced it across his enemy's chest, dropping the soldier to his knees in bloody defeat.

Eric smiled when he saw Brandon conquer his task. He then sailed past Brandon and Matt to an amphibious halftrack vehicle where soldiers were swinging a 30mm anti-aircraft cannon at them. Eric turned to warn his partners, but there was no need. Matt had the aura of a true warrior with blood splattered across his white jacket.

Brandon saw the loader locking a HEDP projectile into the cannon. He knew what had to be done and took off like a bolt of lightning. As the soldier's hand grabbed the firing mechanism, Brandon sliced his sword across the loader's forearm and chopped it in half. Then to make sure the soldier saw death, he stabbed his sword brutally into the loader's chest three times, piercing his lungs.

The soldier screamed in pain. His severed arm was spewing blood and it covered the firing mechanism where the weapon was useless. His fingers were still dangling on the trigger, and then his hand flopped to the dirt along with his bloody body.

Brandon took off past his ailing enemy and was proud of his performance. In the foreground, he spotted Matt and Eric dealing with the others so he decided to take a solo run. His partners could easily take care of things here.

Sailing in and out of the wavy sand dunes, Brandon was having the time of his life. Everything was simply glorious.

A warm breeze flowed through his hair delivering the sensation of absolute freedom. The horse was also enjoying himself. His long snout was snorting feverishly, loving the experience.

But something menacing was waiting for them at the next sand dune.

A large soldier armed with an E4 M-60 machinegun ran to the top of the hill, bracing the firearm like a gorilla. He pulled the trigger and round after round the belted ammunition fed through the upper carriage of the powerful weapon. Feeling the recoil of the gun, the soldier aimed the tracer bullets that shot every three rounds at the oncoming angel and his mighty horse.

Several blazing bullets whisked past Brandon, coming dangerously close to his head. He positioned his body to be out of the line of fire when a tracer nicked the side of the horse's mane and scorched his hair. "Damn you! I'll get you for shooting at my horse," Brandon shouted. He held his sword high, hugged his body against the horse, and they soared indignantly at the soldier.

Unfortunately, the grunt knew how to use the M-60 well. Focusing the 308 caliber rounds at the horse's belly, bullets zipped everywhere as several flaming tracers headed straight at the horse. Right away the animal reared his head back to save both his face and the angel on his back. In war, the horse and rider must become as one.

Hit, then another hit. The horse caught five bullets in his stomach that reared his body backwards with such intensity it tossed Brandon from his back.

Still cruising forward, the horse put his head down in a ramming position and smashed into the soldier. This knocked the grunt to the dirt and flung the M-60 several yards away.

The soldier stood on his feet. The first thing he saw was Brandon coming toward him.

Brandon looked at the wicked person. For some reason this made Lisa flash before his eyes. It was trash like this that caused the world to change and eventually took his lover from him. Years of heartache and sorrow came forth. Brandon told him forcibly, "Now is your time to die!"

The soldier spit on the ground. "Screw you, you angel of God."

As Brandon walked towards him, the grunt pulled out a large revolver and shot several rounds. Gunshot blasts lit the air in a fiery glow. But Brandon blocked the bullets with his chromed sword and kept stepping closer.

By the time the soldier had shot the fourth round, Brandon was standing directly in front of him. With precise precision, he swung his sword gracefully and severed the grunt's hand that held the pistol.

Crying out in anguish, the soldier's blood squirted everywhere.

A stream splashed across Brandon's face, but he shook his head from side to side and then sliced the soldier into pieces, dropping him to the dirt.

Brandon stared at the expired being, but then a heavy pain arose in his stomach. A sharp throbbing had devoured his midsection. He looked down. To his surprise, a sword was penetrating his stomach. Another soldier had run up from behind and stabbed him through his back, which delivered two types of pain: one in his gut and the other in his manhood.

Brandon couldn't believe that someone was able to sneak up on him. Damn that demon!

The newly arrived soldier screamed, "You're going to die now!" and sliced the sword completely through Brandon's body, slashing him like a hot knife in butter.

Brandon felt an excruciating pain devour his stomach. At least fifty-percent of his body had been sliced. And to make matters worse, his favorite jacket was even cut.

A burst of energy flowed through him. Brandon Summers stretched his arms up high and yelled, "Lord, heal me!"

A vigorous sensation of extreme warmth triumphed over him. Brandon looked at the wound. It healed before his eyes. There wasn't even a scar to be found. He smiled but noticed that his jacket was still torn. "Hey, what about the jacket?" he hollered. At that very moment the jacket was made whole, as though the fabric was new.

The soldier that stabbed him stood flabbergasted. How could he kill this angel?

Brandon laughed while basically reading his mind. "You chose the wrong side." He then sliced his sword across the soldier's chest, dropping him dead into a pile of dust.

Instantaneously, Brandon's white stallion flew down and hovered nearby waiting for his commander. The angel hopped on the horse and they sailed into the sky.

While they traveled through the air, the soldier's blood that stained Brandon's face was blown away, washed clean by the wind.

Chapter 58

As the war between good and evil proceeded, the angels were slaughtering the infidels. An angel flew over the marshlands of Florida and noticed movement behind some bushes approximately a mile away. Heading that way, he found the source of the rustling. It was a family: two adults and two children.

The angel landed in front of them, raised his sword to butcher the whole group, but suddenly stopped. He sensed that these people had refused the mark of the beast.

The warrior of God scanned the man's right hand and forehead. They were not stamped. The angel smiled once he realized this family had escaped the wrath of the antichrist by hiding in the woods, the same method of action that many people had chosen. Thankfully it worked out because this looked like a nice family. "Hello, my friends. Stay here. We will be back shortly to take you to paradise and freedom."

The angel flew away, leaving the family mesmerized.

# # #

Hovering over the battle, Jesus was overseeing all things. His eyes were blazing as he sat on his white stallion. His top four warriors, Brandon, Matt, Daniel and Eric, were before him on their stallions. Christ nodded his head to inform them that their assignment was approaching.

Brandon glanced at his old buddy Matt and couldn't believe all the cool things that have happened. Matt was to be thanked for most of it. Without him, Brandon might not have found and stood for what he believed. Therefore he would have missed out on this awesome experience.

Jesus directed, "Brandon, Matt, go get the false prophet. Daniel, Eric, get the antichrist. And bring them both to me!"

The four took off in a flurry, facing the most important task of their existence.

Brandon thought of whom they were going against – the antichrist and false prophet of satan's trinity: the two demons that walk the world. Best of all, his job was to bring down someone he already despised - that heathen Jack Smitty.

The angels cruised toward the earth heading to Israel. Once they reached Jerusalem, the group split out to search for the dwelling place of the evil ones.

Brandon knew that battle was close. He glanced over and spotted Matt spurring his horse trying to locate their opponents as quickly as possible.

Matt, his good friend, was actually beside him to bring down the antichrist's right hand person, the false prophet. Who could have ever known? As the Good Book says, "Behold, there are last which shall be first, and there are first which shall be last."

# # #

The four angels sailed in the clouds above Jerusalem, then Eric caught the rancid scent of his enemies and pointed his sword at a hi-tech building in the heart of the city. The group took his lead and they surged in like a wave splashing against the shores of Malibu beach.

Several armed guards on top of the building saw the angels approaching on horseback. One raised his weapon to kill them, but Eric flew in and hacked him in half, splashing the guard's intestines onto the rooftop.

Brandon smiled from watching the intensity in Eric. That man really loved his job! In the foreground, a guard pointed a weapon at him except Matt reached him first and did his duty.

Brandon sailed on to team with the others, and they soared ferociously at the building.

Chapter 59

Standing in front of a large desk inside a plush office, the President and Jack Smitty were watching the angels slaughter their soldiers. An entire wall was covered with televisions. The middle set highlighted the display of video power, possibly the largest television ever constructed.

Several smaller sets surrounded it, resembling a tic-tac-toe board, and each set aired a different section of the worldwide war. The largest television showed Armageddon.

The President was stunned that he was being beaten, and being beaten badly. It consumed his soul with hatred as he saw his men being butchered. He screamed profusely, "Fuck that God and his army! They're killing ours!"

Smitty stared at the screens in disbelief. They were getting their butts whooped. His usual plastic smile was wiped away as a fearful glare controlled his eyes. He mumbled bewilderingly, "If God's army of angels win, then we shall die forever."

Jeff heard every word. "Shut up, you stupid fool! They'll never take me alive." The President glanced at the screens just as several angels sliced a group of his soldiers in half. He yelled at the monitors, "Come on you pieces of crap! Can't you kill a few stinking angels?"

Jeff picked up a heavy paperweight from the desk and hurled it at the largest screen.

# # #

Eric flew in the air with only one thing in mind: to bring down satan's true son, the antichrist. Holding the horse's reins in one hand, he gripped his sword in the other and soared toward the office building's brick wall. Brandon, Matt, and Daniel were close behind.

Eric's horse put his head down in a ramming position and crashed into the wall like a linebacker breaching an offensive line. Bricks and stones scattered everywhere through the air.

Brandon was getting into it. Excitement was building in his heart. While he prepared to smash through the wall, a warm sensation swallowed his spirit.

Suddenly, a backlash of bricks and stones from where Eric had entered came flying at his face. Brandon dodged his head to escape the sharpness of the jagged bricks, and then they crashed through the wall with vengeance.

Chapter 60

Inside the Jerusalem office, the President was fuming. The paperweight that he threw smashed into the largest television, shattering the screen into a thousand slivers of glass. Then, at that exact moment, the entire wall behind the monitors blew open, exploding the equipment back into the office.

Glass, televisions, and bricks were thrown on top of the antichrist and false prophet, knocking them to the floor by flying debris. They struggled to throw the junk to the side.

But the instant they stood on their feet, they saw the four angels of God standing directly before them.

Smitty became dumbfounded. He didn't know what to do. This plan wasn't transpiring like he thought or like he hoped. He stared fearfully at the angels. Dust from the walls was floating off their jackets. "Oh, shit!" Smitty squealed in panic.

Except the President wasn't going so easily. He was much more crazy and ready for a fight.

Jeff jumped in a solid stance, kicked debris from him and screamed, "Die, you filthy angels!" He pointed his right hand at Eric as a burst of flame shot from his palm, consuming Eric in blistering heat.

Brandon couldn't believe his eyes. Fire was consuming Eric's body. As he was about to jump in to help, he saw Eric through the flames push his sword outward, which bounced the burning hot flames back into the President's hand.

The fire devoured Jeff's hand, making him shriek, "You dirty ass bitch! I'll get you for this."

Eric blew a puff of smoke from his mouth and laughed at him. "You're the antichrist? You're nothing more than a punk boy. And your fire cannot hurt us. For we are angels of God!"

Jeff growled hatefully, then he lunged at Daniel. But Daniel lifted his special sword that shot twelve-inch chrome spikes from the blade. He shot the first spike into Jeff's side, knocking him backwards. Then Daniel popped another beside the first and the pressure flung the President to the wall.

Jeff's body slammed against the hard surface, which threw his arms outward.

Daniel saw the perfect opportunity. In rapid fire, the angel shot four other rounds: one into each wrist that nailed the antichrist to the wall, and one hitting Jeff in each ankle. This hung the demon on the wall as Jesus had hung on the cross.

Daniel smiled at a job well done.

Eric commended his partner on such superb shooting. "Great job, Daniel."

"Check it out, guys," Brandon added. "Daniel crucified him!"

Matt was ecstatic. Watching the antichrist get nailed to the wall showed him that everything he stood for was true and righteous.

Daniel, the prophet of the Old Testament Bible, looked happily at his fancy shooting. "Yeah, man. Twenty-six hundred years old and I still got it. Praise the Lord!" The three angels responded, "Amen."

Smitty looked for a way out. He didn't care to participate in their conversation. The last thing he wanted was to be crucified on a wall to bleed to death. He needed an escape route and he needed one fast.

Searching his mind, Smitty tried to recall if the Bible he always carried was nearby. The inside was hollowed with his Walther PPK, 380 semi-automatic, fit snugly in there. "Oh, damn," he muttered as he remembered he left it behind because the words "Holy Bible" bothered Jeff, that little wimp. Smitty noticed the doorway and dashed toward it, but Matt was much quicker.

Matt tossed a golden lasso rope around Smitty's neck like a prizewinning calf roper.

The moment the rope touched Smitty's neck, it stopped him cold. His upper body froze while his lower part kept moving, resembling a cartoon character. His feet were running but his body was caught and he fell flat on his back. Brandon and Matt jumped on him to tie him up with Brandon's rope.

Rage flared in Brandon as he tightened the rope around Smitty's neck. Jack Smitty was the one who had deceived millions into receiving the mark of the beast, and ultimately eternal hellfire.

Brandon yanked the robe roughly to force Smitty to stare into his eyes. "I always wanted a piece of you!" He then smashed Smitty's face on the ground that burst his nose, spewing blood everywhere.

But Brandon wasn't finished playing with the rat. He yanked the rope violently and slammed Smitty's head once again against the concrete floor.

Blood covered Smitty's face, turning him into a putrid red.

Jeff Christensen was nailed on the wall going crazy with rage. Blood flowed freely from his wrist, ankles and side. Now he saw Smitty being tied up. "Fight them off, you stinking runt!" The antichrist struggled to un-nail himself as he yelled banefully at Eric, "Let me go you piece of God's shit! Or I'll kill you all!"

Jeff's eyes glowed in a repulsive red as he stuck out his tongue and hissed like a poisonous snake at Eric.

Eric looked at the disgusting trash, despising who and what he was. "Shut your nasty mouth, demon." In a quick move, Eric swung his mighty sword and chopped off Jeff's tongue, cutting it completely from his mouth.

The President screamed hysterically. Blood was gushing from his mouth. He tried to speak but coughed pitifully on his own fluid.

Daniel and Eric jumped on the President to bring him down, accomplishing the task in the first take.

Eric wrapped his rope around Jeff's neck and pulled him to the ground. Daniel yanked Jeff's arms from the spikes to hogtie him.

Beside them, Brandon and Matt had Smitty bound securely.

In the blown out section of the wall where the angels had entered, their white stallions flew up and hovered in midair waiting for their commanders to leap onto their backs.

Brandon held the rope tied to Smitty and jumped on his horse while Matt jumped on his.

Eric yanked the rope that held Jeff prisoner but heard a loud snorting sound. He glanced at his horse and got the message. Fun and games could wait, it was time to deliver these fools for prophecy.

Eric leaped through the air, landed on his horse and looked over his shoulder. The image of the antichrist and false prophet hogtied and spitting blood brought him tremendous joy. For some reason this made him recall back to his human years when some of his old acquaintances had laughed at him for accepting God.

But Eric would get the last laugh. After these two demons were delivered, there will be many rewards bestowed unto him and to all the true hearts in the Kingdom.

Angel Eric and his three partners, Brandon, Matt and Daniel, were about to rock-n-roll in paradise!

Eric let out a yell and the four warriors took off into the galaxy with the demons in tow.

Chapter 61

Flying at an immense speed, Jesus made several sweeps through the masses of soldiers just to get his hands wet. He returned to the sky, looked at the battle with satisfaction and spotted his four angels soaring to him triumphantly.

Brandon and Eric held the ropes closely to their sides as they dragged the demons inhumanly. Brandon laughed when he noticed the two repugnant prisoners gagging for air, and he tugged his rope to force Smitty to look at him.

Smitty was gasping for air but found enough strength to yell, "Die, you sorry angel!"

Brandon winked at him just to screw with him more. He then saw Jesus floating in the sky on his mighty stallion. Flying in formation, the four came to a stop in front of him.

Eric stretched his arm forward that held the robe. "My Lord, we have delivered the antichrist unto thee."

Brandon handed out his rope. "And here is the false prophet."

Jesus took the ropes. "Great job, my warriors." He threw his attention to the demons while yanking them towards him. "Come closer so I can see thee better."

Christ stared intensely at them from head to toe. "You thought you could beat me?"

The four angels laughed boastfully.

The laughter drove Jeff crazy. He hocked up a mouthful of lung sludge and spit at Jesus. But it was a zillion to one to actually hit God. Jesus snapped the ropes to the side that flung the demon's face into his own saliva.

Spit splashed in the middle of Jeff's nose, coating his eyes. The demon shook his head from side to side to clear his vision. Blood was flowing from his mouth and he was having trouble speaking because of his butchered tongue.

226

Jack Smitty yelled, "To hell with you all!" Smitty's eyes, along with Jeff's eyes, started to glow in a hideous red.

Christ didn't appreciate the remark, so he snapped their ropes which caused the demon's heads to slam together like airplanes colliding in midair. The antichrist screamed hysterically, "Screw you, Holy One!" Smitty squealed, "Our master will kill you!"

Hearing as much as he would allow, Jesus stated powerfully, "For you greatly err. First, I shall never die. Second, as my word states, the light of the body is the eye. If thy eye is evil, pluck it out and cast it from thee. And your eyes are evil."

In lightning speed, Jesus sliced his fingers across both of their faces and cut their eyes completely out. Their retinas splattered inside their head.

Pus flowed profusely from their eyeless sockets, making the demons squeal in pain.

God yanked the ropes and told his four warriors, "Follow me."

They took off with the demons in tow. The ropes were choking the evil ones half to death.

# # #

Brandon was awestruck after witnessing the most incredible sight he could've imagined. It was impressive when Eric severed the demon's tongue beforehand, but this was the bomb. Jesus sliced out both of the demon's eyes, and he did it with only one chop. How cool!

Brandon smiled. It filled his heart with delight to be on God's side. It certainly turned out to be the wisest choice of his life. If he hadn't made that decision, he could've been one of those slaughtered fools lying on the earth that was about to be burnt to ash.

Brandon realized that his whole existence had been leading up to this, like his destiny was designed from day one of his life. A few feet away Matt was flying in the sky holding his sword high. It was terrific to have his buddy beside him. He always knew this friendship would last forever.

A flickering in the middle of space stole Brandon's awareness. What could it be? It appeared to be a large lake flaming of fire.

At first the glowing lake puzzled him, and then he realized it was the lake of Fire and Brimstone. The place where infidels shall be tormented with damnation.

It was astonishing. The surface resembled an erupting volcano with molten lava oozing deadly smoke and brimstone. Sparks of fire were sparkling all around it.

As Jesus arrived closer to the lake, he began to swing the demons around his head. Twirling them around and around, their screams grew louder and louder. Then Christ let them go. As they soared in the air, their screams grew fainter and fainter.

Jeff Christensen and Jack Smitty, the two gooneys of satan's trinity, flew helplessly into the pit tumbling head over heels. Once they landed in the lake, waves of fire splashed upward hundreds of feet as their screams of pain could be heard reverberating into space. Then almost instantly, the two demons disappeared in the flames. They were burning alive, being sucked under out of sight.

Where they landed, the molten lava burped up a burst of fire as though it had eaten a bad burrito.

The beast was taken, and with him the false prophet that wrought miracles before him, and both were cast alive into the lake of fire burning with brimstone.
Revelation 19:20

Brandon shook his head. It was all so spectacular. Thankfully there were witnesses, who would have believed him? In the distance he caught sight of Matt straddling his white stallion.

Matt's face showed a triumphal glow, a look of supreme happiness.

Now twelve angels flew down from heaven and hovered in the air before Jesus. He proclaimed, "Go instruct my warriors to hold back the birds." At that, the twelve took off to the earth.

Brandon couldn't figure what holding back the birds meant. How could the birds have anything to do with this? His first impulse was to ask, but stopped himself.

He has learned that things were being revealed by themselves and recalled the Scripture, "For there is nothing covered that shall not be revealed." So he decided to wait and see what will happen with the birds, even though the wait would be difficult. But he knew if he didn't find out now, he would in the future.

Immediately following, one of the greatest angels in all of creation was flying down to them. And it was obvious he was prepared for battle. A mighty chain was wrapped around his right hand, showing he was ready to rock!

Brandon couldn't believe the size of the angel. He nudged Daniel in the side. "Hey, Daniel. Check this out. Now that's a big angel."

"Don't you know who that is?" Daniel responded surprisingly. "That's Michael the archangel. He's my buddy, I've known him for over two thousand years."

Brandon stared in awe at the archangel. "Wow!"

Michael threw the heavy chain over his shoulder and stopped in midair before Christ. He waited patiently for his instructions.

Jesus smiled at Michael as he recalled the time when Michael had disputed the devil for the body of Moses and how he conquered prolifically. "Michael, oh Michael, how heaven has loved thee," the Lord thought pleasantly in his mind. He then told him, "The time is at hand, Michael. Go bind satan for the thousand years and place my seal upon him."

Michael smiled as he took off with the colossal chain, now knowing what he must accomplish.

Brandon was dazed, perhaps more confused. Could Michael actually have the strength and power to bind the devil? He was one big and bad angel, but this was satan he was going against. Brandon thought that only God could have the power to accomplish this task. "My Lord, won't it take your strength to bind satan?"

Jesus' words echoed victoriously, "Satan is unimportant. He has nothing. Everything he had, he lost. For all has been taken from him!"

Chapter 62

In the desert outside of Baghdad, the sun set over the horizon at the end of a windy afternoon. Dusk was approaching. Strange noises were sounding in the terrain as a coyote howled dramatically in the wilderness.

The sky glowed in an abnormal shade of reddish orange. Pools of blood and bodies scattered this area and several other parts encircling the world. These were the people who had chosen the mark of the beast and were butchered in the battles. These were the ones that denied God, the ones that chose wrong.

A Jackrabbit ran across the desert scared to death. The past few days have put fear in the little rabbit. With all the guns and cannons going off, along with the bolts of lightning that exploded earlier, the bunny was glad to have some peace and quiet.

Hopping across the blood stained dirt, the bunny was having trouble moving because the liquid was so thick and sticky. He splashed into a thicker pool of blood, jumped high and landed on a soldier's body.

The soldier moaned grievously. He was close to death at any moment. His stomach had been slashed and his guts were hanging halfway out of his body. Then another sharp pain attacked his system, so he glanced down his cutup torso and saw the culprit of his new anguish. A rabbit was sitting on his exposed intestines.

"Damn you. If I wasn't hurt, I'd kill you and eat you for dinner," he groaned. The bunny sensed him and lurched forward by digging its feet deeply in the soldier's wounded stomach.

The soldier threw his head back to yell his misery, and then he spotted Michael the archangel descending feverishly from heaven. The soldier shut up to take the pain. The approaching angel could surely rip him apart in seconds flat.

As the large chain lashed across Michael's back, he searched for the bottomless pit where the demon horsemen had exited from beforehand. It came into view and this meant it was time to fight satan again.

The archangel recalled the first time he battled Beelzebub and how easily he had won. Hopefully the devil had toughened up since then. Michael prayed that this fight would be more of an entertaining battle.

Flying a few hundred feet above ground, Michael picked up movement. It was the heartbeat of the wounded soldier. But when Michael pinpointed him, he knew the soldier would soon be a bird's snack. So he paid him no mind and sailed into the bottomless pit.

Entering the abyss, he violated the invisible barrier. The archangel was crashing into the house of the devil, the dwelling place of satan.

The bottomless pit that Michael had breached was the gateway to the pit of hell.

The ground shook like a major earthquake had struck, rocking the desert so dramatically that sand dunes were leveled flat. As dust filled the already dark sky, everything became totally silent. Now the earth gave another strong jolt.

Black smoke spewed from the hole as demonic screams rumbled hauntingly in the tunnel. Then the screams faded to silence.

Within a few seconds, Michael sailed out of the pit, chainless. Once again he was the reining victor over the evil one.

I saw an angel come down from heaven with a great chain in his hand. And he laid hold on the devil, that old serpent, and bound him for a thousand years in the bottomless pit, that he should deceive the nations no more until the thousand years should be fulfilled: and after that he must be released for a short time.
Revelation 20:1,2,3

The archangel soared past his Lord and smiled cheerfully while heading to heaven.

The joyful glow on everyone's face would show Michael he had done a sensational job. Satan was bound for the thousand-year period, concluding this part of the war against evil.

A massive light began to shine around Jesus, growing intensely like a power was blazing from within. His long hair flowed in the wind as his eyes twinkled robustly. He glanced over the world and was pleased with the job his army had accomplished.

An angel holding a golden trumpet flew down. Christ instructed, "Blow the horn to let my warriors know it's time to come home." He stated pleasantly to his four angels, "Come, my friends. Paradise is waiting."

The horn sounded loudly. Then Jesus and his posse: Brandon, Matt, Daniel and Eric, flew peacefully into heaven.

Brandon rode behind the pack, loving every minute. His heart was happy. This was an experience his wildest dreams could've never produced.

Beside him, Matt was cruising comfortably on his stallion. Matt thought about how pure and alive he felt. Gobs of blood might be splashed across his jacket and pants, but he couldn't recall a time of feeling so good, so clean about himself. The warmth of nature caressed his body delivering a magnificent feeling.

But Matt also knew the Scriptures and realized there was still a large job in store for him and his comrades in the near future. He noticed a lot of activity at his side. Millions upon millions of angels were coming together, all traveling in the same direction. Then Brandon sailed past him. Matt was proud of Brandon's bravery and how he came through as a warrior of God.

Brandon's attention was focused forward on a breathtaking sight.

The Kingdom of Heaven was just before them.

Brandon gasped. The pathway to paradise was totally exquisite.

A large time warp was being sucked through space with beautiful and peaceful colors glistening from the inside out.

Brandon rode his horse swiftly into the lighted tunnel. He felt like the luckiest person alive from being chosen as one of the four inner warriors.

Then his thoughts were swept to Lisa. How could he think he was the luckiest of anything without her?

Even though Brandon was heading into paradise, he knew that without Lisa there would always be a longing in his heart. A hunger that only she could fill.

Chapter 63

Brightness twinkled in the sky, illuminating the horizon in pure beauty. Brandon was captivated as several beaming lights burst beside his head like bottle rockets exploding. Then the time warp expanded and the angels sailed elegantly into the sparkling gates of heaven.

Brandon's hopes were high to find Lisa, especially after he heard there would be a great homecoming, a celebration for those who had conquered the evil.

Wishing with all his heart to find her, Brandon cruised beside Matt into an amazing area.

Jesus flew in, got off his horse and stretched his arms to his massive army of angels. "Great job, my children! And welcome home. The evil has been destroyed and prophecy has been fulfilled for now."

Christ saw the blood stained robes that covered his angels. His voice was caring. "Come, enjoy, for my word shall wash you clean."

Jesus waved his hand in the air and to the angels' pleasant surprise, their blood splashed robes suddenly changed into white tuxedos. Everyone entered paradise with the honor of being a triumphal victor as many beautiful angels flew down to greet them.

The atmosphere swiftly turned into a large celebration of peace and harmony. Friends and families were uniting with happiness filling the hearts of all.

Brandon and Matt got off their horses. Matt was excited to check out all the action.

But Brandon was focused on only one thing, to search for his love. Looking in every direction, he stared at a large field of green grass and saw Eric getting off his stallion. An attractive angel on horseback flew down to greet Eric. She threw her arms around him and embraced him in such a loving way.

Brandon chuckled at what happened next. Eric's girlfriend's horse rubbed its head against Eric's horse. Brandon thought, what a family, horses and all!

The horses flew away leaving Eric with his woman. Eric stared passionately into her eyes, adoring the precious light that danced abundantly in her soul. Their two faces became as one as they kissed tenderly, and then they sailed into the horizon to be together for evermore.

Once Brandon saw this, he longed even more for Lisa. His sight surfed everywhere to find her, but it was useless. She was nowhere to be found.

Brandon put his head down. He sighed deeply.

Matt saw this and felt for his friend. He knew that Brandon's mind was on Lisa so he tried to make him laugh. "Hey, man. Look at you. All dressed up and nowhere to go. Why are you so gloomy? You've never had a tuxedo this nice in your life."

Matt gave him a buddy punch and stepped back a few feet. "You know, the more I look at you in that tux, the more you resemble an ugly penguin."

"A penguin, huh?" Brandon laughed.

"Yeah, and don't get so down. If it's meant to be, it'll happen."

"I guess you're right."

"Of course I am, and look at the bright side. I'm running solo tonight and there's a lot of pretty angels out here." Matt grinned happily. A large smile covered his face.

But Brandon bent his head low. "Yeah, but they're not Lisa. I wonder where my baby is?"

Chapter 64

With a colorful rainbow shining above, Brandon and Matt strolled through paradise enjoying the wonderful afternoon. A few days had passed and Brandon's face showed a smile, but he was confused about Lisa. He couldn't get her off his mind. Thankfully, his favorite pair of blue jeans draped his legs.

God was so cool that he had everyone's most cherished clothes waiting for them in heaven.

Matt walked beside him absorbing the beauty of the lush green pastures. "Isn't this place astounding?"

"It sure is but it's so large. I can't find by baby anywhere."

Matt understood how his friend felt. But it was a shame that Brandon wasn't taking pleasure in this fabulous place like he should. He told him sincerely, "Keep the faith. All things can happen here."

"I know, but I pray that I'll find her soon." The instant he spoke those words, Brandon felt a powerful sensation consume his being. Perhaps now, after he had prayed for it and not just hoped or wished, it was time for it to happen.

As Jesus stated in Mark 11:24, "Therefore I say unto you, what things soever you desire, when you pray, believe that you receive them, and you shall have them." So now it was time for Brandon's prayers to be delivered.

An invigorating breeze blew pleasantly as Brandon looked upwards and saw a sight that made his heart flutter. A stunning vision was approaching.

The love of his life was floating down. Lisa's arms were held open while her dress flowed behind. Jenny, her best friend, was beside her.

Lisa's face glowed of true love as she landed in front of him and whispered, "Hello, stranger."

236

Brandon was spellbound. Was this actually Lisa that stood before him? Or was it another dream?

He stood there just staring at her. Then, as if by instinct, her name drifted off his tongue, "Lisa?"

Lisa stared at her man, ecstatic to see him. So many emotions were surging inside her. She placed her hand on his face and rubbed his cheeks. Oh, how great it felt to touch his skin again. It was like pure ecstasy.

Brandon was finally convinced it was she. "Lisa, it's really you!" he exclaimed joyfully.

"Yes it is, honey. I am here."

There wasn't a moment to spare. Brandon wanted so badly to hold her, to feel her in his own two hands, to grasp her beautiful body, and he grabbed her around the waist. "I've been dreaming of this."

Blood rushed through his body while he picked her up and spun her gently in the air, yelling the entire time, "My baby, my baby!" Brandon placed Lisa back on the ground. All he could do was gaze at her gorgeous face, which caused wonderful memories to flood his thoughts.

Tears started to drip from his eyes. "I've missed you so much."

Lisa wiped away the wetness. "There are no tears in paradise, just peace and love." She leaned close, laid her lips upon his and kissed him with the passion of longing for this moment.

As of this second, there was nothing that could stand between her and her man. Nothing.

Matt and Jenny stood behind them. Matt cleared his throat. "Hey, you two lovebirds."

They heard the gesture and stopped kissing. Lisa blushed. Her cheeks turned a bright shade of red. "I'm sorry."

Brandon couldn't remove his sight from her. It gave him such a rush to see her blush over something as sweet as kissing. He loved it. The foxy mama of his life was back!

"Hey, no problem," Matt stated. He was happy to see his old friend again. "How have you been, Lisa? You look great."

"Thanks, Matt. I've been." She glanced at all of the dazzling sights that surrounded them. "Heavenly." Everyone laughed.

Lisa motioned to her friend, playing matchmaker. She knew this day would come and already had it planned. "Matt, this is my friend, Jenny. I thought you two might like each other."

Matt placed his arm around Jenny. "I know, we've already met. In fact, she was about to show me around this splendid place."

Lisa smiled. She knew they would hit it off. Even though Brandon had always told her not to set up the world, she figured he would make an exception this time. Especially when she saw the glitter in Jenny's eyes when she stared at Matt.

Lisa remembered that she hasn't introduced Brandon. "Jenny, before you go, this is Brandon."

Jenny was delighted to meet him. "Hello, Brandon. I've heard so much about you."

Brandon didn't know what to say. His entire focus was on Lisa. He shrugged his shoulders and responded happily, "Hey, all right. It's nice to meet you, too. I hope you guys have a marvelous time." He grinned at his best friend Matt.

Matt glowed of satisfaction. "Who could've known it was going to be this nice. Hey, Brandon, I told you heaven would be cool!"

Matt gave his buddy a thumbs up and looked at Jenny. Their eyes locked together like two honey bees meeting for the first time in front of a blossoming rose bush. Matt held Jenny's hand and told his longtime friends, "See you later."

Jenny waved at Lisa and Brandon. "Bye-bye." Then, as mellow as two butterflies in the wilderness, Matt and Jenny floated into the horizon hand in hand.

Brandon held Lisa affectionately as he stated, "I can't tell you how good it is to see you. You take my breath away."

"Mine too, I love you so much. And how would you like a personal tour of paradise?"

As if by instinct, their fingers weaved together like silky fabric, two lovers reuniting once again. "If it means being with you, then I would love it."

Brandon was still having difficulty believing this was happening. He could only praise God. At this very moment, his dreams were answered. And he knew that whatever it took him to get here, whatever he had to endure, it was worth it. He now had his better half back.

If Brandon could say only one thing, it would be: "Never lose your dreams. Don't worry about what anyone might say to you or about you. Never lose your dreams. Just go for it."

Ecstatic that this day had finally arrived, Brandon looked at his hand that held Lisa's and squeezed it faithfully. They caught each other's stare, kissed once again, and flew into the brightly colored sky of paradise.

These two lovers were on a trip to share an eternity of happiness, the same type of happiness that Brandon wished for you.

Chapter 65

In the throne of God, John's expression showed extreme delight. He stood beside his angel while wondering what would happen next. And the answer came swiftly.

Jesus knew it was time to send John back home. He leaped through the air and landed in front of him. Christ placed his hand on John's shoulder. "Behold, I come quickly. Blessed is he that keeps the sayings of the prophecy. For all things you have witnessed are faithful and true. They will come about, and there's more that shall happen. Go, John, and put these things that you know of and have seen in a book and deliver them unto the seven churches and the world."

Jesus touched his hand against his beloved disciple's face. "I hope you have enjoyed yourself. May peace be unto you."

In the twinkling of an eye, John was sent back to his own time period.

Arriving on the isle of Patmos in the same location where he was before he had been swept away, John was completely astonished. He looked at the immense dark clouds that hung overhead. They started to swirl around and were blown away, leaving the sky in a rich blue.

A familiar voice came into play. His best friend Isaac called, "John, John!"

John waved at his long time comrade. "Isaac, my friend. I have a fascinating story to tell you!"

Isaac ran swiftly to be by his side. "I don't care about any story, where have you been? I've been looking everywhere for you. You had me scared to death!"

John stared closely at him. Will Isaac and the world believe his story? Will they understand?

He knew that many people would reject what he had seen. Though he hated to see it come about, John knew it would be woe unto those who didn't believe in the words of the prophecy.

After several years of imprisonment on the wretched island of Patmos, John was released. Domitian, the Roman emperor who had him exiled for preaching the gospel, died in A.D. 96. Shortly after Domitian was laid in the dirt, the persecution against Christians ceased and things became somewhat peaceful.

After returning to Ephesus in an area called Asia Minor, which is now modern day Turkey, John spent a lot of time writing the Book of Revelation.

He lived a few more years continually spreading the gospel of Jesus and then died of natural causes. John was the only one of the original twelve disciples that died a natural death.

Judas, the betrayer, hung himself. The other ten laid their lives on the line and were martyred for their belief and testimony in Christ. Four of the ten were crucified on the wood. Legend holds that Peter was nailed upside down because he didn't consider himself worthy to be crucified in the same manner as Jesus. Even Paul, who sometimes was considered as the thirteenth disciple, was martyred for his belief and testimony in Christ. Amen.

#   #   #

Jesus radiated happiness as he watched John being delivered safely to the earth. He was proud of John's bravery and would bless him tremendously in the land of paradise.

Christ jumped in the air, landed beside the altar and saw several angels flying above. He instructed their captains to come forward.

Two angels flew down before him. The one on the right was told, "Go gather my children from where they are hiding." To the other, "After they have gathered my own, release the birds to do what they must." The angels' eyes glistened from their new assignment, then they took off with their armies to embark on an interesting adventure.

Jesus reached into his pocket and pulled out a shiny gold coin. As he stepped to the middle of the throne, he held the gold coin up for all to see.

The twenty-four elders plus the four beasts watched devotedly. Even they didn't know what would come next.

"There is much to be done for our new arrivals," Jesus stated while twisting the coin around his fingers. "But first, look at this coin that I hold in my hand. As of today it is one thousand years old." He flipped it from his fingers.

The golden piece spun out of control, twirling rapidly in the air. "And the next time I see it, it shall be a thousand years more."

The coin tumbled head over heels as it sailed through the earth's atmosphere. Within a few seconds, it crashed into the bottomless pit where Michael the archangel had battled satan.

The golden coin had a mission. It slammed into an old wooden crate, tossing it from side to side. But this wasn't a regular crate, this was the box of God that had his seal set upon the top. The seal was stamped with the number of perfection.

The number was – 777.

The coin rested on top of the container in perfect silence. Other than some loose particles of dust floating in the air, only peace and clam dwelt.

But some noise started to generate from within the crate. A light muffled sound could be heard, and then the box lurched on its side from whatever was caged inside.

Just like magic, the gold coin clamped onto the structure as a bright light covered the box, locking it securely. It could be opened only after a thousand years of confinement.

The ancient coin began to burn brightly in the size of a twenty-five cent piece, exposing a hole that showed the inside of the wooden cage. Fighting, struggling, and havoc reverberated in its interior.

Pure evil dwelt inside the crate.

The devil himself was imprisoned, screeching in pain from losing his two prodigies in the lake of fire. It also showed where Michael the archangel had beaten him badly. He placed his bloody face against the peephole, hoping to see something, anything, except all he saw was darkness.

But a beating wasn't going to stop satan from fighting back. The devil thrashed his body back and forth, attempting to break free.

It was an unachievable task.

The chain that Michael carried in the pit was strapped around him, binding him completely.

Once the serpent stopped struggling to catch his breath, the gold coin supernaturally turned into an unbreakable mirror, forcing satan to stare at himself. It was one of God's ways to punish him even further, to show him how the evil has polluted him.

Except once the devil saw his revolting reflection, he screamed hysterically. It was an image that he despised. In the beginning he was so handsome. But when he tried unsuccessfully to overthrow the throne of God and was cast into damnation, the evil, sin and hatred that flowed in his veins changed him into this – a rotting beast somewhere between a deadly dragon and a slimy lizard, a discarded piece of trash.

Burnt red skin covered his body with open sores oozing pus. Blisters flourished over every inch of his repulsive being.

Satan struggled to un-cage himself as he yelled, "You can imprison me for only a thousand years."

Using every morsel of strength he possessed, he tried to break free, but failed miserably. He knew he was stuck in this pit for a long period of time, a time that shall seem like eternity. But as God's word stated, he will be set free again after one thousand years of confinement. Then he'll show them who they were dealing with.

Satan screamed satanically, "One day, you will bow to me!"

THE END
is Coming…

www.ingramcontent.com/pod-product-compliance
Lightning Source LLC
La Vergne TN
LVHW011323080426
835513LV00006B/174